BRIDGE MAKERS:
BECOMING A CITIZEN
FUTURIST

BRIDGE MAKERS: BECOMING A CITIZEN FUTURIST

APRIL REAGAN

NEW DEGREE PRESS
COPYRIGHT © 2021 APRIL REAGAN
All rights reserved.

BRIDGE MAKERS: BECOMING A CITIZEN FUTURIST
ISBN   978-1-63676-722-2   *Paperback*
       978-1-63730-045-9   *Kindle Ebook*
       978-1-63730-147-0   *Ebook*

*This book is dedicated to an incredible circle of
support for which I'm immensely grateful:*

*my daughter, son, and husband, who teach me about myself,
look out for me, and encourage me to pursue my many interests
while accepting all that comes with it (or gets left behind);*

*my mother and late father, for seeding and supporting
my passion for innovation and appreciation of wit;*

*my sister (coconspirator for all things bucket of cheese
related), Shawn, and my wonderful nephews;*

*my aunt Liz, who has been like a big sister to Teri and me, and all of
my aunts, uncles, and cousins who bring the sweet and savory to life;*

the family I choose in Jeff, Carin, Charlie, and all of the Gaonas;

my dear friends Ann, Amy, Andy, Joe, Joanne, Rachel, Mike, and Liz,

*the teachers who built me up—Barbara Carter, Ellen Wright,
Anton Schulzki, Maria Melby, Bruce Hall (rest in peace), Dr.
Robert Hinks, Professor Halperin, and Dr. Surya Pathak.*

CONTENTS

	HOW TO USE THIS BOOK	11
	INTRODUCTION	13
PART 1.	**THE CALL TO FUTURISM**	**27**
CHAPTER 1.	FUTURES... LITERACY?	29
CHAPTER 2.	THE BRIDGES TO TODAY	41
CHAPTER 3.	MEET YOUR MENTORS	65
PART 2.	**LOOKING FOR FUTURES**	**81**
CHAPTER 4.	LEARNING TO LOOK	83
CHAPTER 5.	WHERE TO LOOK	97
CHAPTER 6.	LOOKING NOW	109
CHAPTER 7.	LOOKING FOR OPPORTUNITIES	131
PART 3.	**THINKING ABOUT FUTURES.**	**141**
CHAPTER 8.	FUTURES THINKING	143
CHAPTER 9.	THINKING ABOUT POTENTIAL	157
CHAPTER 10.	THINKING PREFERABLE	167
PART 4.	**ACTING ON FUTURES**	**173**
CHAPTER 11.	CITIZEN FUTURISTS	175
CHAPTER 12.	STUDENTS AND EDUCATORS	191
CHAPTER 13.	ORGANIZATION LEADERS	203
CHAPTER 14.	POLICY INFLUENCERS	221
	CONCLUSION	233
	RESOURCES	235
	ACKNOWLEDGMENTS	239
	BIBLIOGRAPHY	247

The Bridge Builder

An old man going a lone highway,
Came, at the evening cold and gray,
To a chasm vast and deep and wide.
Through which was flowing a sullen tide
The old man crossed in the twilight dim,
The sullen stream had no fear for him;
But he turned when safe on the other side
And built a bridge to span the tide.

"Old man," said a fellow pilgrim near,
"You are wasting your strength with building here;
Your journey will end with the ending day,
You never again will pass this way;
You've crossed the chasm, deep and wide,
Why build this bridge at evening tide?"

The builder lifted his old gray head;
"Good friend, in the path I have come," he said,
"There followed after me to-day
A youth whose feet must pass this way.
This chasm that has been as naught to me
To that fair-haired youth may a pitfall be;
He, too, must cross in the twilight dim;
Good friend, I am building this bridge for him!"
—WILL ALLEN DROMGOOLE[1]

---

1 Will Allen Dromgoole, *Father: An Anthology of Verse,* (New York: EP Dutton & Company, 1931).

HOW TO USE THIS BOOK

―

This book is written for a wide audience—it may be helpful to consider the following as you approach the piece though.

The Introduction and Conclusion are for all audiences. The rest of the book is organized into four parts:

Part 1 (The Call to Futurism): This part is context-setting, providing key definitions and examples of major innovations of the past and present. It also explains the types of attributes and activities of professional futurists. This is good general knowledge for anyone to possess. Part 1 features Chapter 1 (Futures... Literacy?), Chapter 2 (The Bridges to Today), and Chapter 3 (Meet Your Mentors).

Parts 2 (Looking at Futures) and 3 (Thinking About Futures) include *prescriptive* chapters that detail the frameworks and approaches practiced by those engaged. Find these details in Chapter 4 (Learning to Look), Chapter 5 (Where to Look), Chapter 8 (Futures Thinking), and Chapter 10 (Thinking Potential).

Parts 2 and 3 also feature chapters on *general insights* about our present context and human psychology: Chapter 6 (Looking Now), Chapter 7 (Looking for Opportunities), and Chapter 9 (Thinking Preferable).

Part 4 (Acting on Futures) is broken down by futures stakeholders, providing the most relevant considerations and resources for futures activists: Citizen Futurists (Chapter 11), Students and Educators (Chapter 12), Organization Leaders (Chapter 13), and Policy Influencers (Chapter 14).

Completing the book is a list of resources for continuing on your futurism journey. A number of online supplemental resources will be made available—watch bridgemakersbook.com for more information.

INTRODUCTION

―

Isn't it remarkable we have so many people studying and thinking about the past but so few thinking about the future?

—H.G. WELLS

When I was in fifth grade following a routine eye exam in elementary school, I learned I needed sight correction. I can still remember the moments just after I got my first eyeglasses—leaving the Sears parking lot, I was amazed by the detail of the leaves and branches on the trees. I experienced this phenomenon again many years later, when I took a Film 101 class at DeAnza College in Cupertino—I have not watched a movie the same way since.

This book will provide enough information about futures-thinking that you never look at the future the same.

The sense of empowerment from learning core elements explained in this book will help strengthen your future literacy, allowing you to become a bridge maker in your community. With this, you will become a Citizen Futurist.

THE NEED FOR CITIZEN FUTURISTS

2020 brought the COVD-19 pandemic, an event for which every part of the world should have been better prepared. Other historical events might have had different outcomes had people taken warnings from futurists. Civic and commercial organizations deprioritize investment in preparedness for low-probability, low-frequency events, ignoring even those having the potential for high impact. The businesses that fared the best during the pandemic had forward-thinking visions before it started. We must learn from the pandemic experience rapidly as we face other increasing threats.

Compounding the risk management investment problem, our leaders and idolized innovators lack significant diversity, and many are incentivized only by corporate revenue, political donations, or acquiring personal wealth. It is up to us, an assortment of world citizens who are focused on our collective well-being, on the good of our planet—over profit—to start paying more attention and working to influence our collective futures. There are many global challenges. Civic unrest and cultural battles are amplifying across the world. The equity divide continues to widen. Many important issues require us to come together, engage in civil discourse, and collaborate toward a better future—locally and globally.

This requires *more* people to think *more* about the future, *more* often.

As of this writing, the phrase Citizen Futurist has not taken on a common definition. Breaking it down, a *citizen* is generally accepted as a member, inhabitant, or native of a community or state. Merriam-Webster defines a *futurist* as "one who studies and predicts the future, especially on the basis of current trends," the definition adding that it is someone who advocates or practices futurism (which is, the reference says, a point of view that finds meaning or fulfillment in the future rather than in the past or present).[2] With due respect to Merriam-Webster, the professional futurists I know would reject that they focus on the prediction of a single future; instead, they speculate a number of possibilities. They also have an *equally* healthy respect and knowledge of the past and present.

I offer, then, the following definition for *Citizen Futurist*:

One who is committed to looking—staying informed about scientific, technological, sociological and economic trends, thinking about the potential impacts and consequences of the trends, and acting—claiming agency and advocating for the potential of such advancements to improve the communities of which they are a member.

FUTURES LITERACY

Democratizing the future means empowering every person with the skills and mindsets to take agency in influencing and *creating* the future. "You can change—and you should change—your future; if you don't, you will live in someone else's future," says futurist and author Bronwyn Williams of Flux Trends in South Africa. "You cannot guarantee a

---

2 *Merriam-Webster Dictionary Online*, s.v. "futurist," accessed February 16, 2021.

future," says futurist and author April Rinne, an independent consultant, "but you can contribute to it."

When I speak with futurists, "futures literacy" is received in different ways. Some are concerned it sounds too academic and a bit exclusive, while others think the phrase resonates with the need to build futures-thinking competency through education. To the extent that talking about and creating futures literacy to democratize the future (that is, to make available to everyone—not to make everyone Democrats, as some have mistaken), is useful and incredibly important.

Ask the average person on the street how they feel about the future, and you will get mixed reactions. Some are quick to make predictions or assert their goals, but most admit to not having really thought about it. This trouble with thinking (or *not* thinking) about the future is not new. Humans are not great at thinking about the distant future—we are hardwired to survive in the present. But we can think about our future; it is what separates us from the animals, according to Williams.

It is part of our own animal instinct, however, that tends to make us anticipate with fear; we are wired for survival. Today, while not necessarily fighting death at every turn, we all have opportunities and demands competing for our attention and it is easiest to just focus on what is right in front of us. Many people go with the flow and allow things simply to happen; fewer and fewer people apply thought and analysis to influence future events in a favorable direction. Futures-literacy is the capability needed for doing just that.

The United Nations Educational, Scientific, and Cultural Organization (UNESCO) provides the following definition for *futures-literacy*:[3]

A capability that allows people to better understand the role of the future in what they see and do. Being futures-literate empowers the imagination, enhances our ability to prepare, recover, and invent as changes occur.

Being futures-literate requires a healthy attitude toward change. Our innate tendency is toward consistency and predictability and that which we have experienced before. Research has shown that we treat our future selves as strangers because it is difficult to conceive beyond the present.[4] By choosing not to think about or not possessing the ability to imagine the future, we fear it instead. And as Churchill once said, "He who fails to plan is planning to fail."

Our world is full of futures-literate people who have overcome innate tendencies, looked to the future, and helped us step onto the bridge of change. I call them bridge makers, and they can be found everywhere. You can find them in civic efforts, from our nation's founders to the many fighting for civil rights today. You can find them in medicine, making progress in fighting diseases, increasing our longevity, and improving our quality of life. Today, you can hear bridge-making futurists like Anab Jain, Jamie Metzl, Ryan O'Shea, Nikolas Badminton, and Pablos Holman talk

---

3   "Futures Literacy," United Nations Educational, Scientific and Cultural Organization, accessed February 16, 2021.
4   Colin Schultz, "Some People See Their Future-Selves as Strangers," *Smithsonian Magazine*, October 29, 2012.

about the promises and threats of innovation. They use their platforms to advocate for the envisioning of possible futures, leveraging creativity, and pursuing those futures found to be preferable.

BRIDGE MAKERS

So why "bridge makers"? I find it to be a great multifaceted metaphor for the Citizen Futurist. Physical bridges, probably the first that come to mind, are mechanisms that create connections between two locations. While we typically think of formally trained engineers as bridge *builders*, bridge *makers* emerge organically from communities of all shapes and sizes to facilitate communication and enable the sharing of resources. In music, there is also a term called the "bridge," which has the role of bringing change.

In a 2017 TED Talk, civil engineer Avery Bang shared her experiences in working with rural communities to build bridges, a dream she pursued after seeing that just beyond the lush all-expenses-paid resorts of the South Pacific, many subsistence farming communities had no access to transportation. For these communities, transportation is a critical connection to healthcare, education, and markets. In at least one of the over 270 communities Bang has served in her mission—putting in the work to fundraise, design, source materials, and then manually transport everything to build bridges in remote regions. The new bridge meant that families would no longer have to regularly bury children lost to dangerous crossings in traveling to school, while also saving residents from having to walk hours for safe, potable water.[5] In developed regions, impressive structures represent remarkable engineering achievements, which also create access to opportunities and services for millions.

Rinne and Williams have both bridged multiple disciplines to facilitate better communications and strategic outcomes for stakeholders. Simultaneously understanding the language and context of two or more different perspectives—be they global development and law, in Rinne's case, or marketing, economics, and foresight in Williams' case—a more effective and balanced point of view can emerge and move a conversation or vision forward. Futurist consultants like Rinne and Williams also help bridge an organization with the future through trends analysis, scenario planning, and more. Williams noted that having marketing in her background primed her with the skills of influencing to ensure good ideas can be promoted.

Lastly, the bridge in music; the bridge is an important element used to disrupt the flow of a song, change the melody, rhythm, lyric, or maybe even meaning, so the listener's experience is transformed. The contrast between the bridge and the rest of the song, the back and forth between verse and chorus, provides new information, a new perspective, or melodic sensation. Bridges can create energy and hope. Some of your favorite classic artists probably make great use of the bridge, such as the classics from the Beatles, the Beach Boys, or Queen. Twenty-One Pilots does a beautiful job of using the bridge, often in contrast presumably to illustrate

---

5   *Ted Archive*, "Building Bridges and Connecting Communities | Avery Bang," May 7, 2018, video, 14:58.

the conflict we sometimes manage in our minds, as heard in "Ride." The verses and chorus of "Ride" are punchy and bold, but the bridge reveals a more serious, quieter undercurrent of concern.

All of these types of bridges lend to the bridge making addressed in this book—making connections to bridge communities in a purposeful way and changing the tone of conversation, shifting the tension, and making room for something new to emerge.

The focus of this book is on becoming a Citizen Futurist, but underlying the entire text is a sense of bridge-making.

THE IMPORTANCE OF DIVERSE VOICES
Increasing the number of futures-literate people is not enough; there must be a far more diverse community of Citizen Futurists.

We are arriving at an age in which science and tech will bring humanity to major ethical crossroads, where the potential for negative consequences explodes exponentially. Advances in biohacking are taking flight in a large transhumanism movement that will blur the lines between person and machine. General artificial intelligence will challenge our understanding of the boundaries of life. Quantum computing will fundamentally change our lives—not just bring us new gadgets. If more people do not commit to becoming more educated and involved in the early debates on these topics, the world will change more dramatically than people are prepared to realize or even consent to.

On the scale of products and services, leaving the design and feedback to a relatively small community can lead to undesirable consequences for society at large. While these outcomes ("negative unintended consequences") may not be predictable or even preventable, having a more diverse set of voices in the conversation would arguably mitigate or minimize them. As technology can be found in every part of our lives now, it would be beneficial if more people became engaged earlier in the process, to help spot potential unintended consequences before they happen and to ensure more ethical outcomes. Recent examples of unintended consequences include data privacy issues, system breaches, social echo chambers, fake news, horrific events being broadcast on social platforms, and the use of these platforms as recruiting tools for extremist organizations.

MY JOURNEY INTO FUTURISM
I am lucky to come from a family of gadget geeks. My dad was an avid consumer of tech gadgets, always coming home with the latest—from Pong to the Atari 2600, from the laser disc player to the pocket-sized TV. I am fortunate that even as a young lady, I was shown enthusiastic support when I would place electronic gadgets on my wish lists or save up my allowance and gift money for a Commodore Vic 20 (an early personal computer) and accessories (tape recorder storage and a four-color plotter). I hung out with other nerds and spent my weekends typing up code from programming periodicals. So yeah, I've always been a tech enthusiast! Tech enthusiasm tends to be sourced from optimism about the future. But I have always considered both the good and the bad that comes with innovation.

For school, I wrote about the future of society in 1984, looking to 2001. Written as a diary entry after my recent return from space, I captured these "observations":

- Affordable amenity-rich housing equipped with alien species defense systems
- Public town-to-town conveyor "tracks"
- Both five-seater space commuter shuttles and one-person space vehicles
- Digital news by modem or computer disc delivery (twice a day!)
- Nutritious meal capsules
- Peace between Russia and the U.S.
- No taxes
- Nuclear weapons are banned worldwide

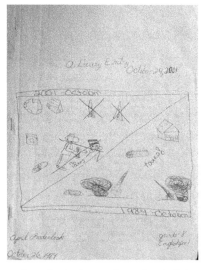

The cover page of my first of several academic futures reports; this one from 1984. I never said I was an illustrator or that I had great penmanship!

During my junior year of high school—1988—I wrote a paper titled, "The Effect of Automation on Employment." The following is part of the introduction, which is a fair parallel to the conversations about artificial intelligence today:

Although it would be somewhat logical to assume that robots will simply replace people in the workforce, the actuality of the situation is that a "skill-twist" will emerge. It is believed that robotics in production will not have a precipitous effect on employment, and the change will appear in staffing patterns. As the demand for machinists, specialized operations, and production-line workers goes down, there will be a rise in the need for engineers, field technicians, computer scientists, programmers, and educators. This shift from a higher-percentage blue-collar to white-collar workers will raise the level of education and training in the average worker's background.[6]

I have worked in high-tech for over twenty-five years now, for companies like Intel, Microsoft, and Samsung. My love for technology had taken me to the Consumer Electronics Show (CES) in 2010 and every year since. It was there I really began to envision futures far beyond whatever product or service I was working on.

---

6   John H. Gibbons, *Office of Technology Assessment: Computerized Manufacturing Automation*. (Washington DC: Congressional Board of the 98th Congress, Library of Congress, 1984).

I always make time to find cute robots like LIKU, from Torooc, at CES.[7]

In 2015, I spent much of my time doing secondary research into a number of topics, such as the sharing economy and technology in education to inform a vision for mobile in 2020. I would spend hours in the Stanford library researching

---

7   "A Robot in Every Home," Torooc, accessed March 23, 2021.

periodicals, journals, and academic literature. In that process, which I thoroughly enjoyed, I became aware of and familiar with the many trend reports published by a number of organizations—primarily market, design, and strategy consultancies.

These reports have become especially common and important over the past two decades. You will find a list of sources of these reports in the Resources section of this book.

It was the Fjord Design and Innovation annual trend report that drew me to work for the agency in 2015; I appreciated that Fjord trends weren't tech-focused. They focused on the fringe of now to give a hint at what would be happening five to seven years out. What I really appreciated about the Fjord report was that it offered clear guidance to companies on what to do about the given trend. At Fjord, everyone in the organization contributes to the annual trends report, which comes from a mix of bottom-up and top-down development. It was my favorite activity to be involved with, the scanning, collecting, and synthesizing that went on simultaneously at our dozens of studios around the globe. I also had the opportunity to work on many strategic foresight programs for our clients.

A BETTER QUESTION

Because science and technology are my primary areas of interest and knowledge, this book will focus on these types of advancements. This does not mean they are more important than economics or sociological progress—or that they can happen completely independent of them. Although this piece may be a helpful introduction into foresight, this is not a deep technical manual. I hope to provide *just enough* information to spark an interest, open your eyes, and inspire you to pull on the threads of your curiosity. I challenge you to take agency, learn to use discernment, and strengthen the skill of informed anticipation.

Each year when I return from CES, friends and family would ask me, "What's the hot new thing that's coming?"

The better question is not "What's coming next?" but "How can we do better and how can we better serve our future selves and society?"

The answer to this question: look, think, and act.

And read this book.

PART 1

THE CALL TO FUTURISM

"The planet does not need more successful people. The planet desperately needs more peacemakers, healers, restorers, storytellers, and lovers of all kinds."

—DAVID W. ORR[8]

---

8   David W. Orr, *Earth in Mind: On Education, Environment, and the Human Prospect*, (Washington DC: Island Press, 2004), 12.

1

FUTURES... LITERACY?

Fundamentally, literacy is understood to be the ability to read and write, along with skills in basic numeracy. The importance of these building blocks for education is well understood but perhaps not the tight connection they have to a thriving society. Concern Worldwide highlights the benefits of functional literacy, including improved health, gender equality, and reduced poverty. The organization notes those who are literate can participate in democracy—those who can follow what is going on can participate in the dialogue. Literacy gets at the heart of people being equipped to gain access to and participate in processes that affect them.[9] During the global COVID-19 pandemic, Concern noted that "with so much misinformation about the novel coronavirus, one of the best—and most cost-effective—responses we have is education, including educating our communities on prevention, symptoms, and what to do if they need treatment."[10]

---

9   Olivia Giovetti, "6 Benefits of Literacy in the Fight Against Poverty," Concern Worldwide, August 27, 2020, accessed March 10, 2021.
10 "COVID-19 is a Humanitarian Crisis," Concern Worldwide, accessed February 16, 2021.

The broader definition of literacy includes having knowledge or competence.[11] When applied to specific domains—such as personal financial literacy—the term refers to being equipped with a particular set of skills; the 2008 President's Advisory Council on Financial Literacy defined it as "the ability to use knowledge and skills to manage financial resources effectively for a lifetime of financial well-being."[12] The World Economic Forum has identified, as part of its New Vision for Education, several literacies needed for the future: scientific, information, and communications technology, cultural and civic.[13] There are also documented efforts to improve health literacy, vaccine literacy, visual literacy, and data literacy.[14]

In the introduction, we considered this definition from UNESCO to help us understand what it means to be futures literate:[15]

A capability that allows people to better understand the role of the future in what they see and do. Being futures literate

---

11   *Merriam-Webster Dictionary Online,* s.v. "literate," accessed February 16, 2021.

12   President's Advisory Council on Financial Literacy, *2008 Report to the President,* Washington DC: The Department of the Treasury, 2008, accessed on February 16, 2021.

13   "New Vision for Education," World Economic Forum, March 2016, accessed February 17, 2021.

14   Ashley Brooks, "Health Literacy: What is It and Why is It Important?" *Health and Sciences,* Rasmussen University, November 18, 2019; Scott C. Ratzan, "Vaccine Literacy, a Crucial Healthcare Innovation," *Harvard Business Review,* February 28, 2011; Sara Briggs, "Why Visual Literacy is More Important than Ever and Five Ways to Cultivate It," *InformEd,* November 7, 2015; Josh Bersin and Marco Zao-Sanders, "Boost Your Team's Data Literacy," *Harvard Business Review,* February 12, 2020.

15   "Futures Literacy," United Nations Educational, Scientific and Cultural Organization, accessed February 16, 2021.

empowers the imagination, enhances our ability to prepare, recover, and invent as changes occur.

In other words, being futures literate is to have the skills and mindset required to participate in processes that influence futures. Let's consider some of these.

THE CHANGE MINDSET

In the year 2020, everyone learned the importance of being flexible. Some people in your circle likely easily adjusted on the fly and others are weighed down in shock and anxiety. Have you reflected on your own reactions to the unexpected or considered why it is that some people are quicker to adapt? Rinne and I caught up recently to talk about futures literacy and this important topic.

In Rinne's book *Flux: 8 Superpowers for Thriving in Constant Change*, she brings three unique lenses to the topic of flux and constant change: those of a futurist, a global citizen, and a human who has experienced profound loss firsthand.[16] Rinne's mission is to help people develop a healthy relationship with change, and you could not have a better mentor. The first funeral Rinne attended in her life was, tragically, at age twenty after both of her parents were killed in an auto accident. After being thrown into flux by this event, she realized a deeper gratitude for being alive. "It is a gift and a privilege simply to be alive. All too often, we seem to forget this and see it as some kind of entitlement. *Yes,* we have a right to

---

16 April Rinne, *Flux: 8 Superpowers for Thriving in Constant Change*, (Oakland: Berrett-Koehler Publishers, 2021).

dignity, humanity, etc. but we don't actually have any right to be alive, so to speak," she wrote in a message following our interview, closing the sentiment by quoting Stephen Colbert: "It is a gift to exist, and with existence comes suffering."[17]

Rinne returned to her passion for global development with a boomerang into law. She lived and worked all around the world, from the slums to the most advanced urban centers of the world. These diverse work and life experiences made her multilingual not just in the languages of word but in the languages of life. Rinne could explain to aspiring social entrepreneurs and venture capitalists the realities of the very context they sought to build business and invest in but which they all too often didn't fully understand (to everyone's detriment). Rinne's book explains how you can unlock the agency you have with regard to the future by taking a deep, honest, and holistic internal look at your own relationship with change. By doing this internal work, we can see change as an opportunity, not a threat.

It is not that people do not like change, as is commonly said. Think about it—we continue buying new clothes, trying new hairstyles, driving new cars, upsizing, or downsizing homes, and so on. These are examples of controlled and anticipated changes (and many driven by consumerism). Anticipation is the key. Otherwise, we are reacting. What we are less comfortable with is anything we did not plan for—especially something we do not understand. Humans are hardwired to be focused on the present, for survival, constantly surveying

---

[17] Stephen Colbert, "Anderson Cooper 360," *CNN*, August 15, 2019.

our surroundings to form our best opinion on how to act.[18] Rinne includes in her book how different cultures have a different way of dealing with change. Certainly, many in the West "are emotionally addicted to certainty," explains futurist Amy Webb, founder of *Future Today Institute*.[19] This natural anxiety about the uncertain future affects how we think.

When confronted with something unexpected, we compare what we see with our memories of the past, searching for times we faced a similar situation so that we might make sense of it—and all in a split second. Our reaction is informed by what we know and understand to be true. I admit my own relationship with change needs some work; my reactions to change varies, like the first reactions of toddlers to a jack-in-the-box toy—either total shock or pure delight (and sometimes a mix of both!).

CONCEIVING OF THE FUTURE
Parents find it easy to imagine idyllic futures for their children, just as people excel at giving other people the same advice they themselves have trouble heeding. But because it is harder to imagine a future for oneself different than what is familiar, we dwell on decisions, procrastinate, and ignore obvious truths about our behaviors. People put off all sorts of things—going to the doctor regularly, investing

---

18 Jim Taylor, "Is Our Survival Instinct Failing Us?" *Psychology Today*, June 12, 2012.
19 Amy Webb, "Amy Webb's Emerging Tech Trends for 2020," May 6, 2020, video, 5:02.

in retirement, letting go of vices, or putting in the work on challenging relationships.[20]

Sometimes people turn to professionals, like motivational speakers Tony Robbins and Brene Brown, in search of fixes for the bugs in their human software, hoping to hack into a futures mindset that can conceive of something more, something better. When we don't accomplish everything we want to, we beat ourselves up mentally because we have a fixed story about ourselves. Some of the techniques taught by life coaches are designed to essentially reprogram the brain, rewriting our personal story by rewiring it, using neurolinguistic programming. Coaches guide us to live more intentionally—that is, to influence our own futures with our actions of today. Most of us know exactly what we should do—eat well, exercise often, maintain strong relationships, contribute to society. But more often than not, we don't follow through. Without a strong *Why*, it can be hard to source that motivation to change. Imagining a better future can help shine a light on and help us to articulate the *Why*.

Even with coaching, the cycle can sometimes continue to feed itself: plan to be "better," eventually "fail," and then admonish our efforts. Don't give up—give yourself a little grace. When it comes to making life easier for our future selves, it is in part because it is hard for us to *imagine* who we will be. Science has shown that we think of our future selves as strangers and that we treat those strangers with

---

20 Joseph Ferrari, "Psychology of Procrastination," American Psychological Association, 2010, accessed February 17, 2021.

little empathy (assigning them a low priority).[21] By creating and visiting possible futures, you build your futures literacy capability and begin to regard your future self as a loved one.

REHEARSING THE FUTURE

One practice that can be used to visualize the future is Mental Rehearsal. In the seventh grade, I wrote a paper on Mental Rehearsal, a technique originally applied to athletics. Mental Rehearsal is when one creates a dynamic mental picture (eyes closed) of going through the exact steps to see and feel the desired outcome: making that free throw, hitting the fairway, landing that triple axel, etc.[22] This technique has since been embraced outside of sports.[23] It can be used for rehearsing presentations, demonstrating leadership, or even surgery; it also has value in psychotherapy treatments of anxiety and post-traumatic stress disorder.[24] Mental Rehearsal has been a proven method for improving the likelihood of success. The process activates muscle memory even though the body is not moving.[25] In February 2018, scientists shared they had learned a bit more on how this works—by getting

---

21 Jason P. Mitchell, et al., "Medial Prefrontal Cortex Predicts Intertemporal Choice," *Journal of Cognitive Neuroscience* 23, no. 4 (2011): 857-66.
22 Jim Taylor, "Sport Imagery: Athletes' Most Powerful Mental Tool—Are You Using Mental Imagery to Maximize Your Sports Performances?" *Psychology Today*, November 6, 2012.
23 Brett Steenbarger, "Tapping the Power of Mental Rehearsal," *Forbes*, February 17, 2018.
24 Lauren Wallace, et al., "Cognitive Training: How Can it be Adapted for Surgical Education?" *The Surgeon* 15, no. 4 (2017): 231-239; Brett Steenbarger, "Tapping the Power of Mental Rehearsal."
25 *Neuroscience News*, "Mental Rehearsal Prepares Our Brains for Real World Actions," February 16, 2018, accessed February 17, 2021.

the brain to the right starting point.[26] Upcoming advances in brain-machine interfaces may provide an opportunity to gain an even deeper understanding of this phenomenon. No matter the scientific reasoning, it is a method that has been shown to work!

CREATING FUTURES MUSCLE MEMORY
How do you rehearse what you haven't experienced? By having the ability to create mental pictures using your imagination. This can be sourced through reading novels, watching movies, or playing video games. The brain cannot discern between memories that come from reality and those that are fabricated.[27] For example, when I was younger, my dad and I worked together on spreading drain rock in the driveway of our Colorado Springs home, and although we were both there, we have different recollections of the work division. This means either one of us was right or the truth was somewhere in the middle (I was right though!). Introducing new ideas and imagery to our brain gives us a store of new information to search for use in a Mental Rehearsal type of exercise.

This need for more information underlines the need to learn about history, too. It is incredibly important, in particular, to try and visualize events to which we were not a witness. Jared Diamond explains, in his book *Collapse: How Societies Choose to Fail or Succeed*, that people forget about the impact

---

26 Saurabh Vyas, et al., "Neural Population Dynamics Underlying Motor Learning Transfer," *Neuron* 97, no. 5 (March 07, 2018):1177-1186.
27 Faith Byrnie, "Remembering Something That Never Happened," *Psychology Today*. July 26, 2013.

of previous challenges faced by their communities as time passes—he referred to it as *historical amnesia*.[28] Not until we were in the middle of suddenly dropping everything to stay home for safety during the 2020 pandemic did most people know much about the 1918 Spanish flu or 1940s polio outbreak.

COLLABORATIVE ANTICIPATION

Besides using Mental Rehearsal to influence our futures, we have to keep our anticipation pay-off table in check. In a well-known experiment conducted in 1972, Stanford professors and psychologists Walter Mischel and Antonette M. Zeis investigated delayed gratification, which used marshmallows for the incentives.[29] Individual children were presented with the scenario where they could receive a small award immediately or wait some time and receive double the award. The initial study explored various factors of the psychology of this future-oriented self-control experiment, highlighting (among other things) that willpower required the ability to distract themselves from the wait—and those who fared well in the test went on to be more capable of managing stress and leading healthy lives. Many follow-up studies have found variances in the effectiveness of willpower based on economic backgrounds or the effect of preceding activities (such as having suffered from a broken promise).[30]

---

28 Jared Diamond, *Collapse: How Societies Choose to Fail or Succeed*, (New York: Penguin Books, 2011), 435.
29 W. Mischel, E.B. Ebbesen, and A.R. Zeiss, "Cognitive and Attentional Mechanisms in Delay of Gratification," *Journal of Personality and Social Psychology* 21 (1972):204–218.
30 Meilan Solly, "Why Delayed Gratification in the Marshmallow Test Doesn't Equal Success," *Smithsonian Magazine*, June 5, 2018; University of Rochester, "The Marshmallow Study Revisited," October 11, 2012.

Perhaps the most interesting follow-up (from my perspective and relevant to the goals of this text) is a recent study, published in 2020, which showed that children can exercise more willpower when acting as part of a team.[31] The study was conducted both in Germany (an individualistic society) and Kenya (a collectivist society). "The results indicate that from early in life, human children are psychologically equipped to respond to social interdependencies in ways that facilitate cooperative success."[32] Despite how different cultures may strengthen or weaken this innate behavior, there is an important seed of collaborative futures literacy that can be nourished in our children.

RESISTING HUMAN INSTINCTS

Building future literacy means being aware of our innate tendencies so we can recognize and try to avoid them when needed. In addition to everything discussed so far, we are wired to be lazy (or extremely efficient, if you prefer)![33] The classic evidence of this in design circles is that no matter how beautifully designed a walking path in a public space might be, if it does not accommodate the most frequently traveled path in the most efficient way, people will tread a new path that does (type in "design versus experience" into your favorite search engine to see dozens of examples). Is a modern example the electric vehicle? Consider those shoppers

---

31 Rebecca Koomen, Sebastian Grueneisen, and Esther Herrmann, "Children Delay Gratification for Cooperative Ends," *Psychological Science* 31, no. 2, (February 2020): 139–48.
32 Ibid.
33 Colby Itkowitz, "Harvard Professor: 'It is Natural and Normal to be Physically Lazy'," *The Sydney Morning Herald*, September 16, 2016.

who pass up the sustainable option because of the perceived hassles of charging.

As part of that efficiency, people sometimes fall victim to the mindset of "it is not my problem." A former manager of mine, Teaque Lenahan, used to say something like "there are latch-and-hook people and there are non-stick-coating people." Latch-and-hook people take accountability and commit to solving it (or finding the right owner), whereas non-stick-coating people deflect problems even at the risk of them never being solved. When thinking about the future, which one of these types are you?

***

Futures literacy, Rinne said, is among the most important literacies for every person on the planet. All told, we have our work cut out for us when it comes to becoming futures literate. Humans operate by instinct and experience. Doing the work to embrace change and uncertainty to live with more intention and informed anticipation is worth it, and necessary, as we will see in the rest of Part 1.

Now that we know the path in front of us is one that comes with many challenges, but ultimately, an invaluable reward at the end, I only have one question for you:

Are you ready to answer the call?

2

THE BRIDGES TO TODAY

Over the past two decades, the rate and breadth of advancements in science and technology have been increasing faster than the rate we can fully process the impacts on our daily lives. This quote from Anab Jain conveys this and more:

Today it can feel like things are happening too fast—so fast, that it can become really difficult for us to form an understanding of our place in history. It creates an overwhelming sense of uncertainty and anxiety, and so, we let the future just happen to us. We don't connect with that future us. We treat our future selves as a stranger, and the future as a foreign land. It's not a foreign land; it's unfolding right in front of us, continually being shaped by our actions today. We are that future, and so I believe fighting for a future we want is more urgent and necessary than ever before.[34]

People worldwide are better off now than they ever have been, though it may sometimes be difficult to see. Advancements

---

34 Anab Jain, "Why We Need to Imagine Different Futures," filmed April 2017 in Vancouver, B.C., TED video, 14:31.

can be used for good or bad; we must pay attention not only to take advantage but to speak up about possible harm. While there exist some "firms of endearment," as Adetayo Adesanya, an engineer with Synopsys, recalled from business school—companies that put purpose and humanity at the center of their mission—most organizations that invest in research and development often have intentions other than to benefit humanity—be that profit, power, leverage, or political advantage. This is not an argument for excessive regulation, but it is a call to action for everyone to be conscious consumers and leaders of purpose. Non-partisan non-profit organizations exist as watch dogs, and we should support them.

THE OPTIMIST VIEW

When asked to consider the one message he would want readers of this book to hear, hacker and inventor Holman said it would be for people to realize that looking on a long-time horizon, everything has gotten better. Save for the recent pandemic, every human on the planet is better off today than a century ago; maybe even a decade ago. Reese, Pinker, and Rosling bring the power of the optimist view to the forefront. Byron Reese asks in his 2013 book *Infinite Progress*:

Is optimism rational? Blind optimism is not, to be sure. If you have an unwavering commitment to an idea that all things will be good all the time, then that is irrational. But what about a reasoned belief based on a balanced look at both history and current reality that leads you to be optimistic? Obviously, that is rational.[35]

Williams spoke to the fact that generally, we live in prosperous and peaceful times; recent shifts to a mindset of scarcity, fear, and helplessness have not served us. Reese, along with authors like Hans Rosling and Steven Pinker in their works *Factfulness* and *Enlightenment Now* (respectively), highlights the optimistic view of how far science and technological advancements have taken us. Perhaps the most striking data point shared by both authors was one from the World Bank—the portion of the world living in extreme poverty (defined as living on less than $1.90US per day, adjusted) has gone down from 84 percent, just 200 hundred years ago, to 24 percent in 1992—and estimated to be under 10 percent today.[36]

Pinker highlights data from the Tanker Owners Pollution Federation, which shows the number of oil spills has dropped significantly since the early 1970s—from an average of seventy-eight per year to today's average of just under seven per year. The size of the spills has gone down as well, the annual average today at 5 percent of the volume in the 1970s.[37] This is remarkable, especially when you consider the *equally significant rise* in oil shipments over the same timeframe.

---

35 Byron Reese, *Infinite Progress,* (Austin: Green Leaf Book Group Press, 2013), 5.
36 Max Roser and Estaban Ortiz-Ospina, "Historical Poverty Around the World," *Our World in Data*, last updated in 2019.
37 Steven Pinker, *Enlightenment Now*, (New York: Penguin Random House, 2018), 132; "Oil Tanker Spill Statistics 2020," ITOPF, accessed February 17, 2021.

Rosling goes on to highlight many global examples of "bad things decreasing," for example:[38]

- Number of children dying before the age of five (from 44 percent in 1800 to 4 percent in 2016)
- Annual deaths from disaster (from just under a thousand per year in the 1930s to under a hundred each year in the present day)
- Cost of solar panel PV modules (from sixty-six dollars in 1976 to sixty cents in 2016)

Rosling also provides pages of data on global "good things increasing," such as:[39]

- Share of people with water from a protected source (from 58 percent in 1980 to 88 percent in 2015)
- Share of adults (fifteen and older) with basic reading and writing literacy (from 10 percent in 1800 to 86 percent in 2016)
- Vaccination levels for one-year-olds (at least one vaccine) (from 22 percent in 1980 to 88 percent in 2016)
- Harvest yields (thousands of kg/hectare) (from 1.4 in 1961 to 4 in 2014)

One reason I love going to CES each year is that the optimism of attendees is palpable. It has been a fantastic routine way to start the new year. Clearly, as a world, we are far better off thanks to innovations in science and technology along with many other forward-thinking policymaking and outreach

---

38 Hans Rosling, *Factfulness*, (New York: Flatiron Books, 2018), 60-61.
39 Hans Rosling, *Factfulness*, 62-63.

efforts. Williams expressed a concern that tech has become the new villain, taking over for oil; she says the change in attitude toward tech since the '80s has been in large part due to its homogenous and limited control of tech. We need to go back to the mindset of the '80s, she says, where tech is not something you purchase and consume but rather participate in and leverage that participation to make the world better.

OPTIMISTIC ABOUT PERSONAL DATA
Data artist Laurie Frick chooses to have an optimistic view about sharing personal data and wants you to, too. Originally working in high tech as an engineer and senior leader, Frick quit to pursue investigating how art might predict scientific discovery. The inspiration was the moment she considered how our time has become increasingly fractioned, and she began the process of measuring time only to realize it was harder than one might think. This fanned a flame of passion for visualizing data, and Frick has since collected all sorts of data and created impressive works that are on display all around the world, including the halls of Texas A&M, The Federal Reserve, Capital One, Marriott, and on the streets of Austin.[40]

Frick uses any and all personal data collectors, collating data sets and analyzing them for patterns. Companies know a lot more about you than you might think, she says, for example:

- How fast you read a book, if you skip pages, or if you just read the summaries.

---

40 "Works," Laurie Frick, accessed March 1, 2021.

- Every video you have ever watched, how long, and how many times
- If you exercise, and the unique gait of your walk
- What projects you are working on—and where

Many of these tracking devices and sensors produce patterns completely unique to you. "What I started to realize, is that this [data] added up to a picture of me that was maybe richer, more complex, or more interesting than I could remember myself," Frick says. Frick was surprised when she first learned the quality of her sleep was not as high as she once thought. This led her to investigate further and make changes to her habits. Many of you may have used this feature of your fitness band, too. The argument for embracing personal data is that sensing, tracking, and analysis can be used to improve and perhaps extend life.

THE DOOMSDAY VIEW

In January of 2020, the Doomsday clock was adjusted to the most concerning time than ever before—one hundred seconds to midnight. And this was before COVID-19 stopped the world. The clock would remain unchanged in 2021 in part due to the pandemic (along with all of the issues noted in 2020, which are discussed below).

The Doomsday clock is the theoretical representation of the level of concern about the risk of catastrophic events like nuclear war, climate change, or disruptive technologies, adjusted each year by a panel of Nobel laureates. Midnight represents the global apocalypse, and the amount of time left is reflective of a countdown clock. When the clock was first created, in 1947, the time was seven minutes to midnight. It would move as close as two minutes to midnight in 1953 with the pursuit of nuclear weapons. Since then, it has moved as far away as seventeen minutes, in 1991, and had been adjusted back to two minutes for two years, 2018 and 2019.[41]

The record adjustment in 2020 was due to a number of factors. "Humanity continues to face two simultaneous existential dangers—nuclear war and climate change—that are compounded by a threat multiplier, cyber-enabled information warfare, that undercuts society's ability to respond. The international security situation is dire, not just because these threats exist, but because world leaders have allowed the international political infrastructure for managing them to erode."[42] Let's take a look at how we've gotten here and contributing factors that futurists were monitoring.

NUCLEAR TECHNOLOGY

Nuclear science is an example of technology that has advanced for the good of humanity (in the medical field) as well as the bad of humanity (nuclear arms). Nuclear energy has good and bad outcomes, with the net value somewhere in the middle; it is a powerful clean energy source (a use that also reduces the number of resources available for weapons) but carries with it the highest level of risk when something goes wrong, as in the widely known story of Chernobyl and the more recent Fukushima Dai-ichi disaster in Japan.

---

41 John Mecklin, ed., "This is Your COVID Wake-Up Call: It is 100 Seconds to Midnight," *Atomic Bulletin of Scientists*, accessed February 17, 2021.
42 John Mecklin, ed., "Closer Than Ever: It is 100 Seconds to Midnight," *Atomic Bulletin of Scientists*, accessed February 17, 2021.

Following this field would require more than one lifetime to see progress unfold, and when key milestones happen rapidly in clusters, it can be even harder to conceive of what it all means for the future.

The field of nuclear physics took a sizable leap when the neutron was discovered in 1932.[43] Understanding in the field dramatically accelerated when, in 1938, physicist Lise Meitner, working with nephew Otto Fritsch, worked out a theoretical explanation for the results of a nucleus-blasting experiment conducted by chemist Otto Hahn and Fritz Straßman.[44] This discovery of nuclear fission set in motion a historical sequence of events, primarily driven by militaristic fervor and including the horrific action of the United States dropping two atomic bombs on Japan during World War II.[45] Meitner had actually declined an offer to join the Manhattan Project, the code name for the US effort to create an atomic weapon, and was "greatly saddened by the fact that her discovery had led to such destructive weapons."[46]

Had this scientific discovery happened at a different time, when the world was not on the verge of war, there may have been more time for the science community to think through the long-term consequences of the application of fission.

---

43 "This Month in Physics History," *APS News*, May 2007, 16, no. 5, accessed on February 17, 2021.

44 "This Month in Physics History," *APS News*, December 2007, 16, no. 11, accessed on February 17, 2021.

45 Valery Nesvizhevsky, and Jacques Villain, "The Discovery of the Neutron and Its Consequences (1930–1940)," *Comptes Rendus Physique* 18, nos. 9–10 (November-December 2017): 592-600.

46 *Encyclopædia Britannica*, Web Edition, s.v. "Lisa Meitner," accessed February 21, 2021.

After World War II, an arms race between the United States and Russia, and a subsequent nuclear build-up, came into sharp focus.[47] Today, the American Physical Society has a coalition of scientists working to reduce the threat of nuclear weapons.[48]

What was the order of events that led to the discovery of nuclear fission? Was there any way the public was aware of the potential impact of this research? There is evidence that society was paying attention, at least at the middle- and upper-class levels, but it is not clear if anyone really knew of the possibilities of what came next. Existing during the timeline below was a lecture culture—some lecturers were authentic, and some were not (perhaps fake news is not so new after all).[49] During the Cold War, there was an active campaign for peace and denuclearization, but the lack of trust between the United States and Russia limited support and instead resulted in decades of Mutual Assured Destruction (MAD) strategy.[50]

---

47 John Swift, "The Soviet-American Arms Race," *History in Review* 63 (March 2009).
48 "Physicists Coalition for Nuclear Threat Reduction," APS, accessed February 17, 2021.
49 "Showing Off: Scientific Lecturing in the 19th Century," *Dickinson College Digital Museum*, accessed on February 17, 2021.
50 John Swift, "The Soviet-America Arms Race."

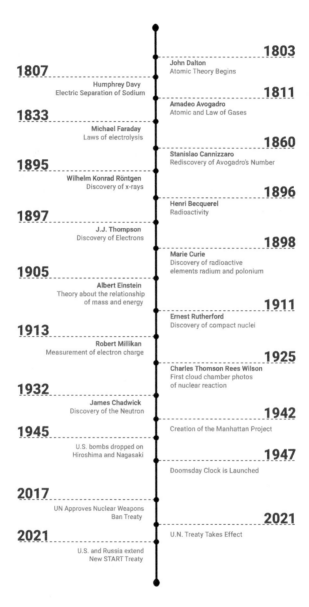

It took just over one hundred years for scientists to make the noteworthy series of breakthroughs and less than two decades for humanity to be at the self-made risk of extinction.

Later, we will look at another field of technology that has an evolution of a similar shape as that of the progression of nuclear science: artificial intelligence (AI). We will look at the progress of AI that also dates back to World War II; we recently have seen clusters of advancement milestones, and society needs to be exercising influence right now before the AI race lands the world in another complex debate (if it hasn't already).

CLIMATE SCIENCE

Most of what we understand of the climate change movement began in the late 1980s, but the investigation started long before that. Early experimental evidence from the 1800s that human-produced carbon dioxide (CO_2) and other gases could collect in the atmosphere and insulate Earth was "met with more curiosity than concern."[51] That changed in the 1950s, when CO_2 data started to be collected and the impact quickly became clear. Confirming the sea would not be able to accommodate the rise, Hans Suess stated, "Human beings are now carrying out a large scale geophysical experiment."[52] So how is the experiment going? A 1988 record has been beaten several times since, and 2020 tied 2016 for the highest temperature year in recorded history.[53] 2020 set records for tropical activity and the number of acres burned from fires.[54]

---

51 "Climate Change History," *History Channel*, last modified November 20, 2020.
52 "A Brief History of Climate Change," *BBC*, September 20, 2013.
53 "2020 Tied for Warmest Year on Record, NASA Analysis Shows" NASA, January 14, 2021.
54 Bradon Long, "Record-Setting Hurricane Season Continues as We Enter Greek Alphabet for Only the Second Time Ever," *Fox43 News*, September 21, 2020. Carolyn Gramling, "Wildfires, Heat Waves and Hurricanes Broke All Kinds of Records in 2020," *Science News*, December 21, 2020.

Journalist Nathaniel Rich explained on NPR's "Fresh Air" that once the conversation in the 1980s was gaining momentum, climate change became a partisan issue as lines were drawn in the sand for and against the oil industry.[55] In between those events, the 2006 film *An Inconvenient Truth* was written and starred in by Al Gore and added fuel to the polarization fire. Then, in 2009, conservatives leaped on an email leak from a research unit in the UK as proof that climate change was a hoax ("climate gate"). The emails contained language that led to confusion regarding the representation of a change in the connection of tree-ring proxy data (a longstanding practice) to global temperatures.[56] Scientists rallied together and issued statements that there was extensive evidence even without that lab's research and conversations that were in question (though still accurate).

Climate science has always been a hotly debated topic. Two major sets of data have been more prevalent in the news than others: global temperatures and the effects of greenhouse gases on the Earth's ozone layer. For the former, the data continues to track a clear warming trend since 1965 and a smoothed trend extending further; a short cooling period from 1945 to 1965 led to a few scientists forecasting long-term cooling, which would potentially cause entirely different

---

55 Nathaniel Rich, "How Climate Change Became a Partisan Issue," *NPR*, April 8, 2019.
56 Robin McKie, "Climategate 10 Years On: What Lessons Have We Learned?" *The Observer*, November 9, 2019; and Jessica Stoller-Conrad, "Tree Rings Provide Snapshots of Earth's Past Climate," NASA, January 25, 2017.

issues.[57] As we are now fifty-five years onward and we continue to see temperature trends warming, that debate stirred by a small number of scientists should be closed.

The effects of greenhouse gases on the ozone have been confusing at times for the average citizen, hearing both of the widely publicized single widening hole over the Antarctic, but also that there are ozone hole seasons as the holes regularly open and close as the climate and weather patterns change.[58] The ozone layer is one of many layers of gases that protect the planet. The facts show that there was indeed a growing depletion discovered in the 1980s, and that it was tied to the increased levels of aerosol pollutants in the atmosphere. There is evidence that policy changes around the world led to a decrease in the pollutants, which allowed the depletion to reverse. In part, it was "increasing public concern over the problem based on the threat of skin cancer" that helped make the global agreement—the 1987 Montreal Protocol—come to pass, says Peter Morrisette.[59] So yes, Citizen Futurist, your voice matters.

With the COVID-19 pandemic, the world had to break from routine practices—and this may give the world a chance to mitigate the worst effects of climate change.[60]

---

57 Thomas C. Peterson, William M. Connolley, and John Fleck, "The Myth of the 1970s Global Cooling Scientific Consensus," *American Meteorological Society*, February 8, 2008.

58 Mike Bettwy, "A Season in the Life of the Antarctic Ozone Hole: A Quarter Century of Satellite Measurements by TOMS," NASA, December 8, 2003.

59 Paul M. Morrisette, "The Evolution of Policy Responses to Stratospheric Ozone Depletion," *Natural Resources Journal* 29, no. 3, (Summer 1989):793-820.

60 Catherine Clifford, "Bill Gates: How the Coronavirus Pandemic Can Help the World Solve Climate Change," *CNBC*, March 31, 2020.

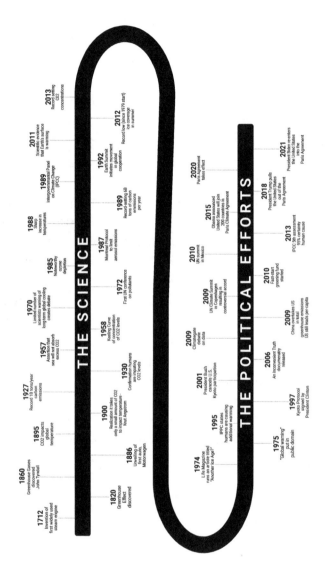

Timeline of events in climate science.[61]

---

61 "A Brief History of Climate Change," *BBC*, September 20, 2013; Jeremy Deaton, "Another Hole in the Ozone Layer? Climate Change May Be to Blame," *EcoWatch*, May 25, 2020; Jess Henig, "Climategate," *Factcheck*,

CYBER-ENABLED INFORMATION WARFARE

The third prong of the justification for the 2020 adjustment to the Doomsday Clock, by The Bulletin panel, was stated as "an information environment so corrupted that it is almost impossible for concerned governments and citizens to mobilize the consensus for necessary action."[62] In this case, a myriad of issues with our digital information systems have provided opportunities for bad actors to launch social influencing campaigns. David Stupples, of City University London, explains that information warfare combines electronic warfare, cyberwarfare, and psychological operations for advanced modern warfare.[63] He states, "Western governments have failed to fully grasp the vulnerability of electronic communications and the enormous risks this poses to critical infrastructure, transport, and the safety of civilians."[64] Cyber-attacks on governments around the world and major commercial interests have littered our news for decades. In February 2021, a cyber-attack on the water treatment site of a small town in Florida, where a technician discovered "someone had seized control of his cursor for several minutes and increased the level of sodium hydroxide—a caustic alkaline chemical used in small amounts to control the acidity of

---

December 22, 2009; Kieran Mulvaney, "When Global Warming Was Revealed by a ZigZag Curve," April 16, 2019; "A brief history of climate change," *BBC*, September 20, 2013; "Discovery of Ozone Hole Announced," *History Channel*, accessed February 20, 2021; Amanda Kooser, "2020 Antarctic Ozone Hole 'One of the Largest and Deepest in Recent Years'," *c|net*, October 22, 2020.

62 John Mecklin, ed., "Closer Than Ever: It is 100 Seconds to Midnight."
63 David Stupples, "What is Information Warfare?" World Economic Forum, December 3, 2015. Accessed on February 18, 2021.
64 Ibid.

water, and in larger quantities in drain cleaner—more than a hundredfold."[65]

You do not have to be a government agent or cybercriminal to take part in information warfare. Other aspects of our modern information systems contribute to instability and polarization in our societies. The content platforms available to all of us yield the prospects for great influential power; unfortunately, it is primarily op-ed in nature and up until 2021 no standards have really been attempted nor enforced. The sheer volume of content the world is generating makes it difficult to ensure the base of every claim is factually accurate. The open internet has completely challenged the traditional genre of journalism. The ability for the world to see live reports from citizen journalists all over the world, especially in areas of conflict, helps the truth get out—but it also provides a medium for extremists to post disturbing content or propagandist material.[66] Today, social platforms, search engine providers, and media companies are working through the challenges of striking a balance between free speech and responsible censorship. Does this censorship even fit with free speech? In the context of a singular service, Holman says it is up to the company to define "safe" content. To avoid this type of censorship, society will have to embrace distributed protocol-based online engagement; this actually used to be more the norm, but given it takes a bit more effort on the side of the citizen, it has not returned.

---

65 "And Not a Drop to Drink a Cyber-Attack on an American Water Plant Rattles Nerves," *The Economist*, February 9, 2021.
66 Kate Bulkey, "The Rise of Citizen Journalism," *The Guardian*, June 10, 2012.

Algorithms on our social networks are shaped to keep people engaged, which typically plays on our confirmation biases and, as Williams says, is optimized for conflict. To design our individual experiences, these companies collect heaps of data about us—often not disclosing the extent to which they track us or profit from doing so. The film *Social Dilemma* attempted to increase awareness of the giant social experiments users have been subjected to, inciting various reactions for the sole purpose of increasing engagements (usually through manufactured conflict). The documentary has come under critical fire in various circles, with claims that the industry speakers were only trying to boast about their personal part of having this giant impact. While I feel there is a lot of value in making more people aware of the inner workings of these platforms, I was disappointed there wasn't more time dedicated to the meaningful benefits that have come from the platforms. It is that which I think creates the dilemma used in the title—the platforms are clearly social experiments given the full control the corporate entities maintain; however, there are endless stories about community building, finding lost friends and relatives, relationship building—especially long-distance—and a clear value in these connections that has kept users there despite several alarming headlines over the years.

Jack Dorsey, one of Twitter's founders, acknowledged the founding group had not imagined the impact it would have on culture, journalism, and politics.[67] The platform, which started as a cool idea of just sharing a snippet of text, evolved to include chatbots deployed specifically to influence public

---

67 TED, "How Twitter Needs to Change | Jack Dorsey," June 7, 2019, video, 25:47.

opinion. Dorsey admits that the original design has led to bad incentivization where the focus is on likes and followers, both of which appear to be metrics that grow primarily because of the entertainment value of negativity and shock value.[68] Sadly, some individuals have made use of live streaming on Facebook and YouTube to broadcast horrific acts—for personal reasons or terrorist intent.[69] Some consumers were frustrated when Ring provided the police access to their video feeds without requiring a warrant.[70]

Without realizing the long-term implications, we began blindly clicking through Terms of Service agreements and End User License Agreements in the '90s—turning over our private data by the late 2000s. With companies quickly finding ways to exploit and expand the data they collect from consumers, data privacy has become a top concern. The European Union's General Data Protection Regulation policies and states like California have made bold moves to make things right. Today there are many proponents for people's right to own and profit from their own data. Apple has long been a walled garden for privacy and has recently taken further steps to rein in app developers on its platforms. Will others follow?

---

68 Ibid.
69 Casey Newton, "How Extremism Came to Thrive on YouTube," *The Verge*, April 3, 2019.
70 Kate Cox, "Police Can Get Your Ring Doorbell Footage Without a Warrant, Report Says," *Ars Technica*, August 6, 2019.

PANDEMICS

New for the 2021 Bulletin of Atomic Scientists report was the reality of the pandemic.[71] The global pandemic was perhaps one of the top two proof cases of information warfare (the other being the repeated interference with elections in many countries). Having disrupted the entire world at a scale many could not have imagined (outside of a Hollywood writer's rooms, video game play, or governmental war games), we are living through the effect of governments and organizations not taking a risk seriously.

In October of 2019, the Global Health Security Index report showed that not one of 195 countries evaluated was fully prepared for a pandemic.[72] Only weeks if not just days later, the world proved this was the case. COVID-19 was declared a global pandemic by the World Health Organization (WHO) on March 11, 2020.[73] By then, the disease discovered only weeks earlier had spread to 110 countries with around 118,000 known cases. As societies quickly became aware of the presence and impact of this new disease, they were forced to make quick decisions about their actions. This brought our health organizations to the forefront.

Both the United States' Center for Disease Control (CDC) and the WHO were founded in the 1940s. The CDC was launched on July 1, 1946, with the primary mission of

---

71 John Mecklin, Ed., "This is Your COVID Wake-Up Call: It is 100 Seconds to Midnight."
72 Elizabeth E. Cameron, ed., Jennifer B. Nuzzo, ed., Jessica A. Bell, ed., "2019 Global Health Security Index," *Global Health Security Index*.
73 Jamie Ducharme, "World Health Organization Declares COVID-19 a 'Pandemic.' Here's What That Means," *Time*, March 11, 2020.

preventing the spread of Malaria.[74] Armed with 400 employees and ten million dollars, they had to find a strategy to wage war with mosquitos. The WHO came into force on April 7, 1948.[75] Each year the world celebrates World Health Day on that anniversary. A primary mission of the group was to standardize disease classifications. The European equivalent to the CDC, the ECDC, was not formed until 2004, after the SARS outbreak.[76]

A relatively small number of countries contribute to the important work of WHO, and in April 2020, just as WHO was in the early stages of handling the largest global event since 1918, the President of the United States, Donald Trump, halted funding to the organization.[77] The justification was the alleged mismanaging of the new disease by WHO. Upon taking office in January 2021, President Joseph Biden reinstated WHO funding.

Many US citizens were quick to recall (but in part mischaracterize) the organizational changes in the Trump administration and ponder how the moves may have contributed to the slow and ineffective handling of the pandemic in the country. The Pandemic Response Unit was formed in 2016 and placed under the National Security Council (NSC) for directives on Global Health Security and Biodefense. After restructuring

---

74 "Our History—Our Story," Centers for Disease Control and Prevention, last updated December 4, 2018.
75 "Milestones for Health over 70 Years," World Health Organization Regional Office for Europe, accessed on February 18, 2021.
76 "ECDC's Mission," European Centre for Disease Prevention and Control, accessed on February 18, 2021.
77 "President Trump Halts Funding to World Health Organization," *CNN*, April 14, 2020, video, 7:33.

done by John Bolton in 2018 shuttered the Global Health Security Unit, its resources being folded in elsewhere in the organization, the unit head resigned.[78] When this happened, the new administration took a lot of heat, but it reassured the public that pandemics were still considered a serious issue. This did not translate to the continued support of Predict, a government research program that focused on detecting new animal diseases that could spell trouble for humans and that lost its funding in 2019.[79]

WICKED PROBLEMS

The four areas we have looked at from a high elevation and through a historical lens are being harnessed to address the "wicked" problems of our global community, which then, in turn, create new "wicked" problems as we have seen here. The "wicked problem" was coined by design theorists Horst Rittel and Melvin M. Webber in 1973.[80] According to the theorists, there are identifiable attributes of the wicked problem:

- Hard to define:
    - A lack of definitive formulation.
    - The uniqueness of every wicked problem.
    - Any wicked problem could be viewed as a symptom of another problem.

---

78 Camille Caldera, "Fact Check: White House Didn't Fire Pandemic Response Unit When It was Disbanded in 2018," *USA Today*, September 10, 2020.

79 Donald G. McNeil Jr., "Scientists Were Hunting for the Next Ebola. Now the US Has Cut Off Their Funding," October 25, 2019, *New York Times*.

80 Katherine Cooper, "Wicked Problems: What are They, and Why are They of Interest to NNSI Researchers?" *The Network for Nonprofit and Social Impact,* 2017, accessed February 18, 2021.

- Any discrepancies in wicked problems can be explained in multiple ways.
- Hard to clearly solve:
  - No stopping rule that determines when a solution has been found.
  - Good or bad solutions rather than true or false solutions.
  - Lack of immediate and ultimate tests of solutions.
  - Solutions are "one-shot" operations rather than trial and error.
  - Lack of criteria that indicate all solutions have been identified.
- Planners have no right to be wrong in that they are responsible for outcomes that result from the actions they take.

Gene Becker, a futurist and a former manager of mine at Samsung, remarked how the futurist community received criticism in face of the pandemic, blamed for failing the world, and somehow considered accountable for the unpreparedness. The foresight community had been predicting and scenario-making (and even gaming) for pandemics for years. Really, it had done its job, and this was a success of the foresight community. They made a case, systems were put in place, but when the threat didn't immediately materialize, some of those systems were defunded and dismantled.

Indeed, Gene made the point that with wicked problems, it is in large part a question of decision making. At the time of our conversation, Gene was a leader of Samsung Research America's AI Center in Mountain View, California. We talked about unintended consequences and corporate responsibility to society, and here is what he had to say:

"To the extent that there are *conscious* decisions that are made, decision-making is diffused into companies that are building products or researchers who were basically pursuing lines of inquiry. For the unintended consequences, nobody makes those decisions, that's an emergent phenomenon that happens across the industry. And it's not to say that those implications aren't necessarily unforeseen; in fact, often they're very much foreseen. But there is no mechanism for having that conversation. Number one, who has it, how do you convene it, and what are the ground rules of that conversation if that happens? Who listens and what's the outcome? It's a very thorny problem. I think you have to, especially for things like these that have such strong ethical implications, you have to have some kind of values alignment. You must decide that there is going to be an ethical alignment, and you must think about *how* do you do work at that level? Because that's the framework within which people will make decisions. What's their value system, what are the things that they believe are good for society, bad for society, or what are the things that maybe they're unaware of and are ignoring?"

Over the past decade, there has been new research into frameworks and approaches for pursuing responsible innovation and uncovering possible consequences. These will be discussed further in Chapter 13: Organization Leaders.

***

There are many reasons to be thankful for the hard work of scientists and innovators who have made the world a better place. There are even more opportunities made available and realized every day. As for avoiding the downsides, the call here is not that everyone needs to become a nuclear-climate-cyber-pandemic expert; but we do need a better system for discussing and creating a set of values that can be used for organizations to plan and make decisions that reflect what the people want.

That is where you come in.

3

MEET YOUR MENTORS

Who better for the Citizen Futurist to emulate than futures enthusiasts and professionals? Whether it's Futurists (capital F futurists—the pros), foresight consultants, strategists, futurologists, gadget geeks, or sci-fi fanatics—there is something to learn from these kin. And who's who, anyway? In 2015, Cartwright set out to create clarity for the terms futurologists, foresight consultants, and futurists. To start, she explains that *futurology* was quite the rage starting in the 1960s, but the term soon came under scrutiny, where most "-ologies" are areas of specific verifiable investigative inquiry.[81] So the term *futurist* emerged, bringing with it less academic stuffiness but also the false impression of predictive and future know-ability. *Foresight* tends to refer to the frameworks and guidelines for thinking about the future.

While there are many different names for futures thinkers, "futurist" seems to be the most appropriate umbrella term, according to Cartwright—even if for some audiences

---

81 Vanessa Cartwright, "Futurist, Futurologist, Foresight Practitioner, Visionary, Foresighteer: What's in a Name?" Ross Dawson, June 2, 2015.

it brings to mind big-stage presentations of fanciful visions and predictions. All of those who pursue various activities seem to agree "there is clearly value in helping people to think usefully about the future," Ross Dawson says, as quoted by Cartwright.[82]

The exponential increase in possible futures that come with record-pace innovation has brought with it an increasing number of futures professionals of all kinds, and for Futurists, there are major professional organizations like the Association of Professional Futurists and the primary pedagogy institute is the Word Futures Studies Federation (a UNESCO partner).

SHARED ATTRIBUTES

In talking with and researching the professionals, I found a pattern of attributes and behaviors that would serve readers of this book. From being insatiably curious to taking pride in creating solutions, these attributes can shape our perspectives and empower us to see the road ahead and act to influence the outcomes—to become futures literate. Individually, these attributes are found in many people, but together they act as a superpower. Let's take a look.

CURIOUS ABOUT POSSIBILITIES

Being curious and paying attention as an attribute may seem obvious, but the sense of commitment to this is the difference. It is reading and listening, attending local and online

---

82 Ibid.

events, with the added step of noticing what is different and wondering how something can become even bigger.

Two friends of mine, Joe Farro and Andy Pennell, have something in common—they both still have the child-like optimism for tech because they love considering possibilities. Early adopters of everything new, they also experiment and hack on electronics and software to create cool things.

Farro is one of the most optimistic people I know (check out his *GeekToolKit* channel on YouTube). With a smile on his face, he imagines things and then brings them to life, from smart mirrors to 3D-printed objects. We often meet up and geek out together at CES. His love for tech goes back as much as forward; for example, he introduced me to the pinball museum in Las Vegas.

Pennell is never afraid to put his skills to work to adopt old and new technology for his needs. One year he figured out how to decode the disc format for a kid's video player to work around a manufacturer issue. Like many software developers, he creates his own Alexa skills when needed and even published an app he wrote to make it easier to use his own Sonos speakers.

Anders Sandberg, a *Future Grind* podcast guest, shared the various ways he stays on top of trends, including stopping by university bookstores in his travels, picking up used textbooks. "I try to at least read the introductions before bedtime. That way, I get a little bit of knowledge about what's known in different disciplines" he told host Ryan O'Shea.[83] O'Shea concludes each podcast by asking his guests a number of questions, including one about how people stay abreast of progress. From pouring over periodicals like *The Economist* to subscribing to key newsletters like Jane Metcalfe's *NEO, LIFE* or Azeem Azhar's *Exponential View*, everyone has a strategy for keeping current. Becker enjoys following the innovation rabbit holes on social media—"curiosity-scrolling"—during downtime.

Your mentors look at the future with excited and curious anticipation. The future does not have to mean the scary unknown; it can mean wonderful surprises. One of my favorite TED Talks is by J.J. Abrams, who talks about the magic of the unknown.[84] In the talk, Abrams shares the story of buying Tannen's Magic Box of Mystery as a youth and how he has never opened it. He hasn't opened it because it represents infinite possibility. It represents hope. It represents potential. He is drawn to infinite possibility. It shows up in his creative work (and I would hazard to guess in how he approaches life).

HOLD A CHANGE-FRIENDLY MINDSET

Stuart Candy, professor at Carnegie Mellon University, in his 2015 TEDx Talk, tells a story about his experience at Burning Man, while taking a shift in the "oracle booth." One help seeker prompted, "Oh, Oracle, I just want to know something about my future."

---

83 Anders Sandberg, "AI, Aliens, and Existential Risk with Anders Sandberg," interview by Ryan O'Shea, *Future Grind*, May 20, 2019, audio, 1:09:15.
84 *Ted Talks*, "The Mystery Box | JJ Abrams," January 14, 2008, video, 18:02.

In response to this, Candy read from Norse artwork hanging in the tent, which said, "Anyone who asks about the future should know that creation and destruction, growth and loss are two sides of the same coin." But then Candy added, "There's a question here for you, too—why do you need to know?"

The help seeker said, "Honestly, because I'm afraid of uncertainty."

Candy responded, "Then the best advice I can give you is to befriend uncertainty."

Change is contextual and relative. What feels like major turbulence on a flight likely depends on what type of turbulence you have experienced before. If you have flown from or to the West via Denver International Airport, you likely encountered a decent amount of turbulence over the Rocky Mountains. If you have taken a "puddle-jumper" on a short flight, you experienced a different kind of bumpiness. For the traveler of more calm airs, either of these would likely be scary if not terrifying. Change feels more dramatic when you're fighting to survive. If you'll recall Maslow's hierarchy of needs, physiological and safety are the base needs for everyone. Only once those are secure can one focus on belongingness and esteem needs, or even self-actualization.

Cecily Sommers, one of Forbes' top fifty female futurists, talks about fighting your resistance to change by employing a "but"-buster technique.[85] Recognizing that "buts" slow the flow of creative problem solving and flag discomfort, Sommers suggests addressing the underlying concerns head-on. By naming and responding to implied blame, denial, fear, avoidance, inaction, or resignation, you can quickly resolve resistance and regain momentum. In Design Thinking, we discourage the use of "but" in collaboration and in brainstorming, as it kills the momentum in the room; we encourage people to say "yes, and..." instead. An oversimplified example could be that instead of saying "But it can't move fast enough to do that," you might say "Yes, and we design it so that it can move fast enough."[86]

When COVID-19 took over the world, forcing it to a screeching halt, changes across all levels of that pyramid of needs happened rapidly and individuals and organizations responded in a myriad of ways. In the year following the start of the pandemic, a library's worth of material was written on the impacts to society and how some fared better than others. It is true that municipalities with more flexible strategies and companies that had made early bets on the future were better positioned to address an increase in scale and changing services. Psychologists have only just begun to see the impacts on people's mental health and medical professionals are concerned for the long-term health of COVID-19 patients as well as those who have put off critical care. Every person had that moment of panic when they coughed or felt a bit fatigued, wondering if they had contracted the virus.

---

85 Blake Morgan, "50 Leading Female Futurists," *Forbes*, March 5, 2020; Cecily Sommers, *Think Like a Futurist: Know what Changes, What Doesn't and What's Next*. (San Francisco: Jossey-Bass, 2012),230.
86 Ibid.

Globally, millions of people died directly from or due to complications of COVID-19, and their families were traumatized by saying goodbye over video calls.

It is worth the time and energy to plan for uncertainty.

An important thing about having a change-friendly mindset is learning to love being uncomfortable. I've repeated the wise words of many women before me when coaching and mentoring others: "get comfortable being uncomfortable." But as I spoke to futurists, there was something slightly different in their message. It's the essence of moving forward even with uncertainty. It means being okay with failure and mistakes, recognizing them as learning opportunities. This is where the creative juices come in—you can imagine things differently, going better, and not fixate on the frustration of the present. In Chapter 13, I share some suggestions to shift your thinking about change, from Jason Clarke, founder of Minds at Work.

NURTURING OF CREATIVE IMAGINATIONS

Candy said, "I think the most powerful idea of foresight is its point of departure…. The future does not exist, it hasn't happened yet—it's not set; it's not predetermined… and therefore the most useful way to think about it is that it's a landscape of possibilities… futures are plural, not singular."[87] To imagine and create multiple futures, you must have developed the reflex and skill. Pursuing creative hobbies and practicing

---

87 *Tedx Talks*, "Foresight 101. Designing Our Own Futures | Stuart Candy | TEDxBlackRockCity," January 9, 2015, video, 15:19.

problem-solving not only builds the creative muscle but provides rehearsal for employing it.

Sommers' journey to futurism was made in unexpected turns through careers as a ballerina, a chiropractor, and a brand strategist. Now a well-respected consultant who works with executive teams to position their brand and business for the future, Sommers appreciates how the combination of art and science is an advantage in foresight. She knows that a range of experience and knowledge casts a wider net for important insights and ideas:

If our capacity for prediction is limited by what we already know, then the solution is to know more about more things. We can't beat the brain's hardwiring, we've got to recruit it by routinely introducing new information, people, settings, sensations, and experiences to expand our data bank of memories.[88]

Nikolas Badminton, futurist speaker, consultant, and podcast host, also sees common roots between his interest in the "edgy wild, edgy edges of thinking." He told me how he has always been drawn to counterculture, alternative and industrial music scenes, and sees his interest in futures rooted in that part of his DNA.

Adesanya prioritizes giving back to underserved communities by producing STEM events, because he knows the importance of nurturing the imagination. He notably opted to become an MBA engineer, rather than continuing down

---

88 Cecily Sommers, *Think Like a Futurist*, 72.

the path he started with the NBA, seeing his own preferable future.

With the STEM programs, it is the experience that matters most, Adesanya says. "The education is secondary, it's still very important, but for me, the most important thing is exposure—even just for them to know it exists, that's step *zero*, and then from there, allowing them to be curious about it, to find a passion, *that's* step one," he explained in our interview. He designs the events in a very intentional way, "allowing them to tinker and get the opportunity to see, to hear and to do, and those three methods play into a lot of kids' learning styles."

ACTIVE PROBLEM SOLVERS

In the face of COVID-19, problem solvers shone. They took to their action-oriented inclination to make a difference. People like my friend Farro made use of their 3D printers to create face shield components for health workers. Anyone with a sewing machine or even a T-shirt and scissors got to work making masks—and taught others how to do so.

As natural problem solvers, futurists think and act a little differently, too. This was the case of James Chadwick, the physicist who reported the existence of the neutron in 1932.[89] Born to a working-class family living in Manchester, England, Chadwick was fortunate to have a teacher recognize his talent and point him in the direction of physics.[90] After

---

89 *Encyclopædia Britannica Online*, s.v. "James Chadwick," accessed February 19, 2021.
90 "This Month in Physics History," *APS News* 16, no. 5, (May 2007).

earning his master's degree at the University of Manchester, Chadwick traveled to Germany to study with Hans Geiger at the Technische Hochschule in Berlin. Still there when World War I broke out, Chadwick soon found himself in a civilian prison, where he remained for four years. You can put a man in prison, but you can't take the scientist out of the man; Chadwick convinced guards to supply him with a toothpaste on the market that also happened to be radioactive, and with it, he carried out experiments with it and tin foil.[91]

Holman is a hacker, inventor, and technology futurist with a unique ability to distill complex technology into practical tools. Always building the future, his projects include cryptocurrency in the 1990s, AI for stock market trading, building spaceships at Blue Origin for Jeff Bezos, the world's smallest PC, and 3D printers at Makerbot. He spoke with me about how he sees himself as having a superpower and enjoys leveraging that power to attack big problems. Industry and governments tend to ignore big problems, so he goes after them through Intellectual Venture Lab and other projects. One project included solving for safe transportation of vaccines to rural communities in extreme locations.[92] Holman spoke with me about tackling the right problems, "we need to make better decisions on what to panic about," he said. Along those lines, in the opening of his TEDx UCSD talk, he spoke about it this way:

"This is really important. I'm only here to tell you not to make any more fart apps for iPhone. The world is trying this grand

---

91 Ibid.
92 *Singularity University*, "Pablos Holman | Automating Ourselves | Global Summit 2018 | Singularity University," September 16, 2018, video, 32:57.

experiment every day of your life, right, we are living in it. The experiment is, can we keep more people alive, every single day on one planet. More people, no additional planet."[93]

It was how Adesanya solved his own problem that created the spark of interest in electrical engineering. Wanting the best sound system in his car in high school, he carefully matched a new amplifier with his recently purchased subwoofers. After encountering some bumpy roads, they suddenly stopped working. He had to disassemble and debug the problem; after successfully soldering a loose connection, he was hooked. He learned this problem-solving mindset from his mother, who drove him one hour each way during middle school to ensure he attended a top-ranking school system she discovered on the news. Eventually, they moved to the least expensive housing in the zone so he could stay enrolled and take advantage of those opportunities, like electricity classes. He credits the general spirit of Nigerian moms, who believe and expect their children to achieve, academically and/or athletically. She recognized early his love of tinkering and equipped him with the tools (like a soldering iron) to do so. Adesanya and his three siblings excel today in part because their mom had the bridge-maker mindset.

TAKE PRIDE IN BEING PART OF THE SOLUTION
Being an active problem solver may be another obvious attribute, but perhaps not the level of pride that comes with it. This mindset can be employed on any given day. Curt Aumiller,

---

93   *TEDx Talks*, "Inventing the Impossible: Pablos Holman at TEDxUCSD," June 4, 2013, video, 16:48.

an industrial designer, shared a story with me about a time when his team was working on a new product. The team was given little notice to produce a demo for an upcoming conference (a scenario that likely sounds familiar to just about anyone in tech). Knowing they had the company's brand and reputation at stake or could negatively impact the product launch, the team leadership was of course, hesitant to rush into putting one together. But a futurist-thinking person like Aumiller was proud to accept the challenge, get to work to make it happen, and in the end, pull it off with great success.

The mindset can also underlie big moments in time. When Jane McGonigal was in her first year of graduate school at UC Berkley working on her PhD, she had a major moment of discovery.[94] She had previously been part of a community of gamers that had an alternate reality online collaborative game called *The Beast* in years past. The group reconvened to try and solve the mystery around the events of September 11, 2001, using their global networks, collective intelligence, and collaboration skills. She noticed this interesting phenomenon, that these gamers felt uniquely skilled as gamers to make a contribution; this was a signal to her. She said, "Play games and save the world."[95] Today, working with the Institute for the Future, McGonigal helps people and organizations develop games that create positive outcomes to problems she is proud to help solve.

Becker also takes pride in taking part in future-forward thinking and activities. He explained to me how he had been

---

94 *Ted Talks*, "Gaming Can Make a Better World | Jane McGonigal," March 17, 2010, video, 20:31.
95 Ibid.

a participant in one of McGonigal's games at Institute for the Future, *SuperStruct*—a massive multiplayer game for forecasting the future. McGonigal's site reports they had 8,000 future forecasters, five super threats, and one Global Extinction Awareness System.[96] McGonigal definitely takes pride in using gaming for good. You can check out an assortment of incredibly cool projects over the last two decades on her website, including her latest effort to help individuals be better—*SuperBetter*, for which she also authored a companion book called *SuperBetter: The Power of Living Gamefully*. This project is particularly meaningful for McGonigal, as it was inspired by her own concussion recovery experience.[97]

Games McGonigal directed also include a 2012 effort with Oprah, the *Thank You Game*, and a 2011 project, *Find the Future*, done with the New York Library, through which coordinators leveraged the efforts of 500 authors over one evening to create a book called *One Hundred Ways to Make History*. The entries include future-looking scenarios along with poems and quips, art and photos; scenarios include a ten-day-per-year tech ban and an affordable solution for custom clothes to meet the needs of the now varied-appendage human of 2060.[98]

O'Shea, an entrepreneur and futurist speaker from Pittsburgh, as a youth was fascinated about the future—drastic changes to humans and society, where we would overcome aging and disease, live with automation and robotics,

---

96 Jane McGonical, "Games—Play Me," accessed February 19, 2021.
97 Ibid.
98 Ibid.

perhaps living off Earth. He told me he thought he would not live to see these types of advances. He was more than just a little bit excited when he learned that some of these things are plausible today. Now, he takes pride in being part of the problem-solving work happening in his industry—so much so he launched the *Future Grind* podcast to bring more truth and optimism to the public than was being promoted by shock-value media. O'Shea currently serves as an advisor and spokesman for Grindhouse Wetware, an organization focused on technology that augments human capabilities. A large part of this industry is the biohackers who are self-experimenting. "Everyone has a role to play in the future, not just certain people with specific backgrounds or knowledge."

FORMATIVE EXPERIENCES

When I spoke with O'Shea, I asked him about the common attributes he finds in the many incredible futurists he interviews for his podcast. The first thing he mentioned—and this held true through my own interviews—is that futurists have been shaped by world travel. Having the opportunity to explore and see the world in a new way, in a different context, brings an incredible new perspective. Second, he noted that many have experienced significant loss (family member or close acquaintance) early in life, changing their view of the world, their values, and their sense of what is important. These people had a shock to the system, a sudden shift in thinking that prompted them to regard the future in a new way. Consider Rinne's story.

At least two futurists I spoke with also talked about the rise in the use of psychedelics in some circles; it is well documented that Steve Jobs had his own related life-changing experience. I expect these will be on the rise, with legislation to legalize some forms being considered in various places.

***

Bridge making is about connecting communities, changing the vibe, being optimistic, and taking pride in the pursuit. Becoming a Citizen Futurist requires some of these attributes to have the open mind and creativity to imagine the future and to back it up with the passion to make it happen. The truth is, all sorts of people think about the future in different ways and to different ends. These are but a few of their stories and shared attributes, and more are to be discovered ahead.

Which futurist attributes do you see in yourself?

PART 2

LOOKING FOR FUTURES

"A signal is something that catches our eye, something strange and unfamiliar that we don't see, it provokes our curiosity and imagination."

—JANE MCGONIGAL[99]

---

99 *SxSW EDU*, "Jane McGonigal | SXSWedu Keynote | How to Think (and Learn) Like a Futurist," March 9, 2016, video, 1:08:59.

4

LEARNING TO LOOK

———

You have probably already done a lot of looking, not regarding it as *futures* looking; some new product caught your eye or you noticed something different in your routine—perhaps you noticed certain types of businesses and services gaining traction. Maybe you manage your own financial portfolio and have even started a business based on what you saw. As Arndt Husar, UNDP strategist, said:

The gray-suited bureaucrat that I am is no longer the one making the decisions. It's the people sitting in a cafe with their laptop or their mobile, deciding on the investments they're making and the new companies that they're starting, disrupting the economy.[100]

This chapter will help you leverage those instincts and expand the ways in which you are looking.

---

[100] "The Use of Strategic Foresight for Adaptive and Future-Ready SDG Strategies," UNDP Global Centre for Public Service Excellence, July 17, 2018, video, 2:54:12.

SCANNING FOR SIGNALS

Futurists tend to call the act of looking around scanning for signals. What is a signal? The term signal is borrowed from electrical engineering, where the primary wave is separated from noise. Merriam-Webster adds "something that conveys notice or warning."[101] With future foresight, Webb talks about framing and then discovering, looking beyond obvious trends to see what is new on the fringe.[102] The UNDP calls this exploring "sensemaking in complexity."[103]

Business visionaries like Bill Gates, Jeff Bezos, and the late Steve Jobs have each leveraged their ability to spot signals to create next-generation products and services. Scanning for signals is something that successful fashion designers must do, as well as interior designers and architects, and a host of other disciplines.

LOOKING LENSES

James H. Gilmore wrote a book called *Look: A Practical Guide for Improving Your Observational Skills*. In the book, he offers six ways to change your perspective to see what is really going on around you. The first three are most useful in our hunt:[104]

---

[101] *Merriam-Webster Dictionary Online*, s.v. "signal," accessed February 16, 2021.

[102] Amy Webb, *The Signals are Talking: Why Today's Fringe Is Tomorrow's Mainstream*, (New York: PublicAffairs, 2016).

[103] "The Use of Strategic Foresight for Adaptive and Future-Ready SDG Strategies," UNDP Global Centre for Public Service Excellence.

[104] James H. Gilmore, *Look: A Practical Guide for Improving Your Observational Skills,* (Austin: Greenleaf Book Group Press, 2016).

- **Binoculars looking:** surveying and scanning from a distance. Use this when considering areas you are already immersed in—take a step back and look at the bigger picture occasionally. I find this is one benefit of going to CES; most of my years in tech, I was hyper-focused in one particular area. Going to CES, I could see the broader industry and its wide-reaching impact.
- **Bifocals looking:** comparing and contrasting. This may be helpful when you have a gut feeling that something is changing but you cannot find anything obvious. Compare and contrast over time, in different locations, and how different generations are behaving.
- **Magnifying-glass looking:** pausing and pinpointing. I like to use this when, similar to above, I have an instinct but just can't put my finger on it. I will peel back the layers of the onion until I get to the core, looking more closely than ever. This lens makes me think of cleaning. Sometimes when I am really deep cleaning, I start seeing every speck of dirt or smudge and it feels like I will never get it all. Once I step away and come back, I realize how in the big picture, it looks remarkably better.

It is not just one lens that you should use—try them each out to unlock more observations and thinking.

LOOKING PILLARS

Scanning for signals is taking an intentional look at trends. It can help to get your mind going by thinking about key factors. "Scanning can be frustrating without containers to sort to," Williams says. Business strategists, who traditionally refer to this as environmental scanning, have used any number of acronyms to cover bases in strategy formation. Most common in this type of analysis are variations of what I learned while earning my MBA, STEEPLE: PESTLE, PESTLIED, PESTLED, SLEPT, and PEST. In these acronyms, the categories include:

- Social
- Technological
- Economic
- Environmental
- Political
- Legal
- Ethical
- International
- Demographic

Williams and the team at FLUX Trends, of South Africa, have adopted TRENDS: Technology, Retail & Marketing, Economy, Natural World, Diplomacy, and Social-cultural—pillars for what they believe to drive futures.[105] Williams explained to me that the Retail pillar is unique and has proven to be valuable in their trends reporting. Badminton relies on FORCEPTS in his consulting practice—Financial, Organizational, Regulatory, Cultural, Environmental, Political, Technological, Social.[106]

Sommers' model is based on the fundamental forces that shape society: Resources, Technology, Demographics, and

---

105 Dion Chang, "Trend Release: The State We're In—6 Trend Pillars for 2021," FLUX Trends, accessed February 16, 2021.
106 Nikolas Badminton, "Consulting," Nikolas Badminton, accessed February 16, 2021.

Governance. As she frames it, since all trends can be traced to these Four Forces of Change, we know how to trace early signals of how they'll mature and spread over time. What's more, the dynamic relationship among the four forces helps make sense of our place in history. For example, we can see them at work in the interdependent techno-socio-economic-political transformations carried by the three industrial revolutions in the twentieth century—first (mass manufacturing and transportation), second (mass communications and computing), and third (internet and digitization). Similarly, the Four Forces are used to forecast implications of the fourth industrial revolution shaping the twenty-first century (convergence of AI, genetic engineering, quantum computing). It takes stepping back and looking at the big picture to make these kinds of connections. [107]

I present all these examples not to overwhelm you but to provide you with options. Typically, one set will make more sense to a person than another, and they stick with it for the long term. But if these models do seem confusing or overly complex, there is one more that might be useful. Ken Gosnell takes a business strategy look with the four S's: Shifts, Starts, Substitutes, and Signs.[108] While they stemmed from an established business framework called Michael Porter's Five Forces, I think these terms might be easier for the Citizen Futurist to remember and to make use of, when generalized.

---

107 Cecily Sommers, *Think Like a Futurist: Know what Changes, What Doesn't and What's Next,* (San Francisco: Jossey-Bass, 2012), 3.
108 Ken Gosnell, "Environment Scanning: How CEOS Can Stay Ahead of the Curve and Beat the Competition," *Business.com*, January 24, 2020.

- **Signs:** Look for external changes, in your local community or with organizations you engage with.
- **Shifts:** Look for your own shifts in mindsets and attitudes—has your comfort level changed with any products or services you use?
- **Starts:** Have you tried something new? Have others, too?
- **Substitutes:** What previous alternatives have become your first-choice go-to's?

Clearly, futurism and looking for signals isn't just about innovation or science and technology—it is as much about human behavior as much if not more. Fjord, a design agency that was acquired by Accenture Interactive in 2013, has consulted on Living Services, which includes liquid expectations—the phenomena where an experience in one context heightens the expectations of experiences in other contexts.[109] An example is mobile ordering—many people first used this option at Starbucks, and after it became familiar, they began to expect to have the option for other dining establishments or retail stores. Once the pandemic took hold, this became a standard.

This expectation level setting can happen in many ways, as Baiju Shah explained in a 2015 article in *The Economist*:

Another example of how liquid expectations take hold is embodied in Blue Apron, which curates recipes based on your dietary requirements and sends hand-picked ingredients that can be made into a meal. This demonstrates how the increasingly popular subscription model is being applied, with expert

---

109 Baiju Shah and John Green, "How Marketers Can Deal with Disruptors," *Fjordnet*, May 20, 2015.

curation, to a new sector creating an experiential competitor for restaurants and fresh local grocery stores.[110]

Since 2015, the subscription model has also been extended to curated clothing and accessories, dog toys, home decor, and more.

Another example of liquid expectations in *behavior*, which I have often used, is the story from a colleague. Her daughter, who interacted with touch-based tablets from a young age, got very frustrated one day when she wasn't able to interact with her TV in the same way. She wanted to be able to swipe or tap and get information and that's just not how it worked, so she was very disappointed.

And I admit there have been more than one instance of me trying to unlock the front door of my house with my car fob!

The acceleration of change that we have seen in the era of the COVID-19 pandemic provided many more examples. Chances are many readers tried, for the first time, grocery or restaurant pick-up and delivery, curbside pick-up for retail, online training options, video conferencing with family and friends, virtual doctor visits, and more. These types of changes happen all of the time, just usually at a slower and less obvious rate.

---

110 Ibid.

CRACKING YOUR BIASES

The way we look at the world is altered by the lenses we unconsciously use regularly. There are dozens of these types of natural cognitive biases that may impact our ability to successfully look around us, behind us, and toward possible futures. Within the context of futurism and looking for signals, it is important to keep these in check, particularly the following:

- **Confirmation Bias:** Detecting a trend might be compromised if, at its core, it simply confirms something we already believe to be true. Humans prioritize any information that matches their existing perceptions of the world—and this can happen outside of political discussions. For example, if you really love your electric vehicle (EV) then you will be sensitive to detecting a trend of increased numbers of EVs on the road or the number of charging stations available, etc. It may be true, and if you are aware you may have this bias, you can check the data before declaring it a trend.
- **Frequency Illusion Bias:** Sometimes referred to as selective attention and more formally known as the Baader-Meinhoff Phenomenon, you might have experienced this the last time you bought a pair of shoes you thought were so unique (only to then see many people wearing them soon after).
- **Self-Serving Bias:** This bias may color your vision if the trend you are detecting serves you in some positive way—perhaps you work for a company that benefits from the trend, or you have stock in that particular industry. As with the confirmation bias, you may still be seeing a

trend, but it is important to see what the data says before running with your observations.

- **The Curse of Knowledge:** This is generally applied to the concept that once you know something for a length of time, it does not occur to you that other people do not know it. For signal scanning, I suggest this comes into play for those who tend to adopt new products and services earlier than the general population. If you have had various smart home experiences in your day-to-day life for years now, you may miss the signals that show these experiences are being democratized (made more generally available through lower cost and broader access). This can be muddled with other similar biases like sunk cost (we don't want to think our investment has been wasted) and negativity bias (we hate to lose).
- **The Decline Bias:** This is an important one in the context of futurism as it is a bias toward the past being better than today (and certainly where we are headed). This reflects back to earlier chapters that emphasized how humans do not like change. If you find yourself thinking that something has become worse, follow that thought further—what exactly is changing? What else is changing as a result? What are the positives and negatives of this change?
- **The Fundamental Attribution Error:** Typically this is around attributing blame, but I want us to consider the possibility of attributing something we see happening to the wrong cause. When people stocked up on toilet paper in 2020, the shortage that resulted was from the panic created online, not because there was a change in the toilet paper supply chain.

- **The Forer Effect:** Sometimes referred to as The Barnum Effect, this is a bias that we all fall victim to as it is hard-wired in our brains. In lieu of information, we fill in the gaps. This can be how we answer the question "Why is this person not responding to my text?" or applying the daily horoscope. We tend to fill in and bend information to have a meaning that makes sense to us, based on our existing perceptions, beliefs, and information we do have. This is related to the discussion earlier in the book about how it is difficult for us to imagine the future if we do not have a lot of ideas to pull from. With regard to signal scanning, it is important that we consider if we are making assumptions about some aspect of a promising signal, and either asking more questions or checking the data.
- **In-Group Bias:** Particularly in today's social context, this is a very important bias to reflect on. As the name suggests, our brains may favor confirmation of information about our own group. Traced back to days of survival where we were wired to protect our tribe, this bias can lead us astray when considering signals that are only true for one class of citizen—geographic, economic, ethnicity, gender, and so on. A common relevant example is tech-adoption tends to be higher in tech hubs; what is commonly available or consumed here may not even be available in other cities or states. You can see where this may lead to false interpretations of what we observe. The antidote, as with other biases, is to check the data. But make sure the data you are checking is not also biased in some way.

Our human brains are subject to many kinds of biases; our search for signals should include a healthy amount of critical thinking and consideration before we declare something to be true. You may be asking yourself; how can I check the data? Which data? Because this answer is so contextual, it is in part an exercise for the reader; you will need to check your sources and search for the best information available to you.

We also need to be mindful of our generational blind spots. We can sometimes miss solutions to old problems; our day-to-day can be relative because—you may have guessed it—our past experiences and expectations limit our thinking. Many I have worked with keep up to date by talking with their teens about trends happening in their social circles; what apps are popular, what do they talk about and care about? Today's teens are more informed on current events and are quicker to form opinions on issues than those in decades prior (in part due to the Information and Digital Ages they have grown in). Magician Synn began her exploration of digital implants after her daughter showed her an article.[111] Coworkers can be great sources, even for me; this is how I first came to learn about Venmo, some time ago. After going out to lunch with work colleagues, someone offered to pay the bill if we would all Venmo them our share—I was the one who had to ask "What's *Venmo?*"

CHECKING HORIZONS

There is one additional type of theoretical lens I would add to Gilmore's set—the rearview mirror. In order to know what is new, you must be knowledgeable about what happened in the

---

[111] Anastasia Synn, "The Magic of Biohacking with Anastasia Synn," interview by Ryan O'Shea, *Future Grind*, audio, 41:30.

past. The ongoing protests and expansion of the Black Lives Matter movement have led people to look back in history at other civil rights movements. I have seen more of my own circle of family and friends begin looking more critically at their biases and lack of education around the lived experiences of minorities in our country. With Black Lives Matter, more people than ever have taken some action—many standing on corners with signs, when they never had before. People, like my daughter, are trying to be bridges to the future—on their own or part of the movement.

Many foresight frameworks include looking at the past, some from an anchor of the present and others from one in the future. When looking at the past, how far back should you look? When anchoring from the now, the availability of historical data and clarity of interpretation for that hindsight can vary by context. Focus on the history of the factors you believe are showing a shift and determine their relative arcs in history. As we saw in Part 1, World War 2 was the beginning of many important innovation arcs. When anchoring in the future, look back to today as well as intermediate milestones.

When you start to consider what may be coming, it is important to consider how far out your speculations go. Within the next year? Two to three years? Eight to ten? Thirty or fifty? Institute for the Future draws the line at ten years. Badminton guides his clients looking across the five, ten, and twenty-plus year horizons.[112] As Citizen Futurists, these general

---

112 Nikolas Badminton, "Consulting."

bands are useful for long-range thinking. The International Futures Forum recommends a Three Horizon framework:

> "The central idea of Three Horizons, and what makes it so useful, is that it draws attention to the three horizons as existing always in the present moment and that we have evidence about the future in how people (including ourselves) are behaving now."[113]

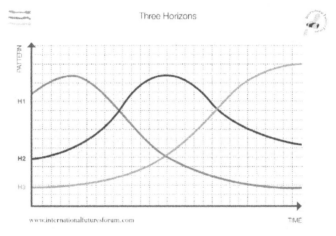

IFF's Three Horizons illustration (used with permission)

The act of looking is figuring out what exists in the first horizon (H1). The bigger changes are out in the distant future on the third horizon (H3). In between these two, there will be smaller changes and transitional steps (H2). The first practice in utilizing this framework is searching for patterns, looking for systemic changes rather than those resulting from specific

---

113 Image © *International Futures Forum*, "Three Horizons—The Approach," accessed February 16, 2021.

events—the consideration of which qualities of our experience today will evolve and expand over the next two horizons.

But wait, aren't horizons about *thinking about the future*, not *looking at the present*? Looking *back* can be just as important as looking around and looking ahead. The horizons are not only falling in front of us but also behind us. Understanding the maturity arc of an area of innovation can help us estimate where it is going. When it comes to signal-detecting, how do you know if something is truly *new*? It can be hard to tell, at times; consider if products and services are *available* but have no real uptake or application.

***

Looking is an area where no two futurists shared the same story, but here we looked at some key strategies you can pull from. Did you know that looking could be so complex?

Once you start to see differently, you will think more clearly about the world.

5

WHERE TO LOOK

In the last chapter, we looked at signals, the various ways we can intentionally look for them, the horizons to consider, and some biases to be mindful of. In this chapter, we will look at the many ways you can look more passively or actively.

PASSIVE SCANNING

Keeping up, in detail, on any domain is more than a full-time job. Still, it is important to prioritize some time in order to stay ahead of conversations. The good news is that you can look during your day-to-day activities. How you approach your daily tasks and activities is where innovation and change can be seen. More specifically, they can be seen in common consumer experiences like payments and banking, shopping for groceries, clothes, and household items, safety and entertainment in the autos you drive, communication with friends and family, or the ways you take care of your children, elders, and pets. For example, home automation products and services have been around for decades, but today they are more accessible, customizable, and personalized than ever before.

ENTERTAINMENT

What is particularly useful about entertainment is that it shows innovation in the context of a narrative—that is, as part of the fabric of an experience and story, rather than innovation for the sake of innovation, tech for the sake of tech.

Film

From the earliest episodes of *Star Trek* to modern series like *WestWorld*, from movies *Back to the Future* to *Ex Machina*, sci-fi has been a wonderful source for visualizing the future. A common provocative reference is the 2002 movie *Minority Report*, which painted a dystopian view of advertising and surveillance. Besides being known for its early picture of the invasiveness of ads, the explorations of human-machine interaction and the various modalities it represented have been centerpieces of inspiration for many of the innovative experiences today. *The Net* also gave an early look at a digital world and increased difficulty in discerning who to trust.

Her showed how our emotional selves might not be able to make a distinction between real and manufactured affection. The *Black Mirror* series has brought a host of topics for discussion and debate and is a rich source of provocative futures. *Inception* is currently the top-ranked sci-fi movie in IMDB's top 250 films list.[114] This film explores the possibility of "a future that allows people to exercise some control over dreams with some training—and experience entire lifetimes

---

114 "Top Rated Movies Top 250 as Rated by IMDb Users," *IMDB*, accessed February 19, 2021.

in one sitting."[115] *2001: A Space Odyssey* and *War Games* gave us early glimpses at working with artificial intelligences like HAL 9000 and the W.O.P.R., respectively.

The fantastical futures illustrated in sci-fi sometimes seem just that—like fantasy; comedies show what real life might actually look like with innovation. There have been comedies that featured awkward interactions with smart homes, like in *Parental Guidance*, or with snarky domestic robots, like Number 7—the digital butler—in *Benchwarmers*. '80s films like *Short Circuit* and **batteries not included* gave us a glimpse at living with lovable robots.

Action and drama genres have their contributions to creating futures as well. Gadget geeks are familiar with the rich resources of major franchises. The earliest Bond movies featured seemingly unusual gadgets from Q like the remote-start car and phone with a display (both from *Tomorrow Never Dies*) and the jet pack (*Thunderball*) but also features ridiculous gadgets like the bagpipe flamethrower (*The World is Not Enough*).[116] The Jason Bourne series gave glimpses of high-tech in security and surveillance, and *Mission Impossible* movies provided us with real-time face-recognition enabled contact lenses (*Ghost Protocol*).[117]

---

115 Rico Mossesgeld, "The Dream-Sharing Technology of Inception," *Tom's Guide*, July 20, 2010.
116 Attila Nagy, "10 *James Bond* Gadgets That Actually Exist—And One That Needs To," *Gizmodo*, December 17, 2012; Jordan Hoffman, "23 of James Bond's Most Memorable Gadgets," *Popular Mechanics*, October 15, 2012.
117 Jordan Hoffman, "The 10 Best 'Mission: Impossible' Gadgets," *Popular Mechanics*, June 23, 2018; Sean Captain, "Mission Impossible: The Ridiculous Tech of Jason Bourne," *Fast Company*, August 2, 2016.

Animation

Somewhere in the mix, you have to consider animation! When it comes to robots, I admit that I have a figurine of Rosey, *The Jetsons'* domestic robot. My son adored the *Iron Giant*. The world of *Wall-E* has prompted some interesting discussions, given the immobility of people and an Earth destroyed, particularly during the pandemic and among climate change discussions. *The Simpsons* has been credited with a lot of prophecies, intended or otherwise, including autocorrect fails, FaceTime, NSA spying, and the 2020 experience (complete with a pandemic and killer bees!).[118]

No matter your favorite genre, film and animation are forms of entertainment that help us think about the future.

Books

As with film, there are any number of resources that consider the future. The vast choices of sci-fi series alone should satisfy the need for creative curiosity. Some are in the very distant future and some are not so far-fetched. According to various 2020 science fiction book rankings, two highly acclaimed recent novels include:

- *The Oracle Year* by Charles Soule: Soule, a comic book writer for Marvel, presents the story of a man who has a rich dream of 108 future events that actually start happening; because he shared information about the events

---

118 Megan McCluskey, "17 Times *The Simpsons* Accurately Predicted the Future," *Time*, last updated June 3, 2020.

anonymously, there are a lot of people interested in finding the source.[119]
- *The Punch Escrow* by Tal M. Klein: This story takes place in 2147, where advancements in science and technology include reengineering mosquitoes and the existence of teleportation. According to Brian Truitt of *USA Today*, "[T]he book posits an intriguing future that is both inviting and horrific" and "digs into the inherent philosophical and ethical questions behind some of these inventions."[120] Rumor has it that Lionsgate has picked this up, so it may be a movie you can check out in the next few years.

HOSPITALITY
Theme Parks

For the United States, Disney's Epcot has always been a futuristic experience, and it has been going under modernization over the past few years. The new experience will include a virtual space elevator and space station. Previously, and now outdated thanks to innovation, Epcot featured "modular, low-cost housing; networked homes; renewable energy sources; automated warehouses; and self-driving electric cars." Other Disney experiences are also future-focused, like Tomorrow Land and Discovery Land. Just visiting one of Disney's parks may be something new for you. Disney's

---

119 Futurism Creative, "These Recent Sci-fi Books Should Be at the Top of Your Reading List," *Futurism*, January 16, 2019; Charles Soule, "The Oracle Year," CharlesSoule.com, accessed February 22, 2021.
120 Futurism Creative, "These Recent Sci-fi Books Should Be at the Top of Your Reading List"; Brian Truitt, "Book Revie: The Punch Escrow," *USA Today*, August 1, 2017.

guest experience is often industry-leading, greatly simplified with the MagicBand, which provides access and payment capabilities. Of course, Disney's parks located around the world also have incredibly innovative features.[121] There are also amazing parks under Universal, LEGO, 20th Century Fox, and other brands, and unique experiences like Futuroscope in France.

Travel

One of the biggest benefits of travel is expanding your mind. Holman explains that he gained a new perspective from traveling. "I'm so enriched by the fact that I get to travel, and I get to go all over the world. You learn to appreciate other cultures. I might not want to live in those places, but I know that my thing isn't better; it is just different. It's not wrong—just different." Cultures create the society that works for them and (in most cases) those differences are to be respected.

Taking a note from Disney, Princess Cruises rolled out the Medallion experience a few years ago. Instead of the MagicBand, you receive a medallion, which you can wear in different ways. The medallion provides access and payments, like MagicBand, and it also enables interactive experiences with various displays around ships, provides location information so you can navigate and find friends or family more easily.[122]

---

121 "Unlock the Magic with Your MagicBand or Card," *Disney*, accessed February 22, 201; Jamie Biesiada, "Evolving Epcot," *Travel Weekly*, accessed February 22, 2021; Chad Nykamp and Cindy Nykamp, "The NEW Epcot—Everything You Need to Know About the Transformation of Epcot," *Disney Lists*, accessed February 22, 2021.
122 "Princess Medallion Class," Princess Cruises, accessed on February 22, 2021.

These ships use a custom network—MedallionNet—to handle all of the traffic and to provide better internet.[123]

Yotel, with a few locations in the US, is a global hotel chain that offers modern experiences that include concierge and luggage-storing robots.[124] Marriott includes digital customer care, and JW Marriott Marco Island includes its own band, which provides access to exclusive sections of the resort for its biggest VIPs.[125]

At CES 2020, held in Las Vegas, there were plenty of photos on social media of robots delivering essentials to guests. Delta took CES 2020 by storm with a booth and keynote showing off a number of new innovations in their roadmap, including door-to-door luggage handling and personalized signage in the airport.[126]

The list of cutting-edge experiences you can seek out are endless—driverless shuttles in Las Vegas, robot baristas that brew your favorite coffee drink in Austin, or robot bartenders that pour you a cocktail (Royal Caribbean Cruises).[127] According to *Forbes*, the smartest cities in the world include London, New York, Paris, Tokyo, Reykjavik, Copenhagen,

---

123 "MedallionNet® The Best Wi-Fi at Sea," Princess Cruises, accessed on February 22, 2021.
124 Yotel HQ, "Hotel or YOTEL?" November 15, 2019, video, 0:31.
125 Marriott, "Find Your Personal Retreat at Our Marco Island Beach Resort," access February 22, 2021,
126 "CES 2020," Delta Corporation, accessed February 16, 2021.
127 "AAA Free Self-Driving Shuttle Pilot Program," AAA Hopon Las Vegas, accessed February 22, 2021; "7 Robot Baristas That Will Make You Coffee," *Nanlyze*, March 23, 2019; "Robot Bartenders Shake Things Up At Sea," Royal Carribean, accessed on February 22, 2021.

Berlin, Amsterdam, Singapore, and Hong Kong.[128] For US high-tech destinations, I would add the cities of Austin, Seattle, Atlanta, and San Francisco. Internationally, I would also add Seoul, Berlin, Dublin, Dubai, Taipei, Stockholm, and Shanghai. Several of these locations boast the world's top internet speeds or have quickly growing innovation hubs.[129]

ACTIVE SCANNING

EXPOSITIONS

Part of your travels could be to visit a special event. For me, the annual CES event is now routine. Some people make attending the Olympics a must-do. The Olympics have become a futurist showcase in their own right. The world at large has long been fascinated with the future, visiting World Expositions since 1851. The first, the Great Exhibition, was held in London. Here in my adopted hometown of Seattle, the Space Needle and nearby Monorail are iconic remnants of the 1962 World's Fair. The most recent event was a specialized fair on energy, held in Kazakhstan in 2017. The last world expo held in the United States was in 1984, in New Orleans. Normally taking place every two to three years in recent decades, plans for a 2020 Expo in Dubai were put on hold given the pandemic but remain tentatively in place for Fall 2021 through Spring of 2022.[130] The theme will be "connect-

---

128 IESE Business School, "These are the 10 Smartest Cities in the World for 2020," *Forbes*, July 8, 2020.
129 Mindy Wright, "Revealed: Countries with The Fastest Internet Speeds, 2020," *CEO World Biz*, February 21, 2020.
130 "Expo 2021 Dubai Main Highlights," Expo 2021 Dubai, accessed February 22, 2021.

ing minds, creating the future." Expos are also planned for 2023 and 2025 in Buenos Aires, Argentina and Osaka, Japan, respectively. The former will focus on creative industries in digital convergence and the latter will focus on "designing future society for our lives."[131]

There are experiential projects out there to help shift our thinking through experience. Anab Jain, mentioned earlier in the book, runs a London studio called SuperFlux that has worked with a number of organizations to create experiential exhibits. In late 2019, SuperFlux provided one of a home in Singapore that shows the reality of impacts from climate change in the year 2219.[132] The Empathy Museum provides incredible live exhibits like A Mile in My Shoes, which gives you a chance to step into another life by donning a pair of donated shoes or Human Library, where you can pick someone to converse with.[133]

Keep an eye out for special events like these in local conferences, colleges, libraries, and museums.

PUMP UP THE FUTURES THINKING IN YOUR FEEDS
In the chapter Meet Your Mentors, keeping current was noted as a common need for the curious. The quality of your feeds will reflect the quality of the curation. I encourage you to check the ratio of the trivial to the important. "There are a lot of things for humans to do and we squander our time

---
131 "All World Expos," BIE Paris, accessed February 22, 2021.
132 "Mitigation of Shock (Singapore)," Superflux, accessed February 22, 2021.
133 "A Mile in My Shoes," Empathy Museum, accessed February 16, 2021; "Human Library," Empathy Museum, accessed February 16, 2021.

on Netflix when we should be taking care of humans," says Holman. "Pandemics are the thing that scares us the most," Holman told me. He explained how Gates tried to raise a warning sign to get people to work on the threat proactively, but it didn't work. When on the Valuetainment podcast, Holman said "I looked in March, just as the pandemic started [Bill's TED Talk] was at 5M views; it's now at 31M—perhaps if a Kardashian spoke about it...."[134]

According to *Friend or Follow*, as of today, the top twenty Twitter accounts (based on followers) are 65 percent entertainment celebrities, 20 percent media brands, and 15 percent non-entertainment public figures (Barack Obama, Narendra Modi, and Bill Gates).[135] By comparison, the US Senate has only fifty thousand followers, and the US House Budget committee only has fifteen thousand followers. We must be mindful of where we invest our time.

It is also important to take control away from algorithms. Algorithms are generically a set of steps and rules in an automated process, but the term has become shorthand for the specific implementations on social media used to serve up content based on your behaviors and habits. Consider personalizing and customizing the settings to ensure your feeds are based more (or completely) on your wishes and not only those of the algorithms set by big tech. As discussed in Chapter 2, many social media platforms prioritize what will

---

134 Pablos Holman, "Futurist & Hacker Reveals How to Solve World's Biggest Problems," interview by Patrick Bet-David, *Valuetainment*, October 23, 2020, video, 1:17:41.
135 "Twitter: Most Followers," Friend or Follow, accessed on February 22, 2021.

help boost engagement rather than what you need to feed your brain, but often turning off the algorithms is just a click or customization away. Or you can always just go old school; Holman told me he still relies on RSS feeds, aggregators, and readers for his news surfing. He and Williams shared that the work in staying up to date is really in filtering and curating, and including history, as it plays a vital role in understanding macro trends. "Consume what you seek, not what seeks you," Holman added.

Take the time for intentional curation of sources into your normal (or new) habit of following the news and enjoying entertainment. There are quite a lot of choices when it comes to finding forward-thinking organizations to follow. From tech journalists to agencies, from design agencies to research groups. There are many mentioned in this book—check the Resources section at the back for a comprehensive list.

O'Shea brought up important points about this curation process. "The best way to make progress today is to make connections between domains, between guilds. That cross-pollination is where innovation occurs. To really have an impact, you need a broad set of input. Break out of the silos that algorithms put you into. Follow accounts of outlets or individuals that would not normally be fed to you, to make sure you are getting this broad spectrum of information, through which you can make connections and initiate collaborations. Find the people that you know will share something interesting in their field, so you don't necessarily have to go looking."

***

The act of scanning for signals can be intentional or incidental, passive or active. The more information you gather, the more you will have to work with in considering futures and awareness of candidate solutions for problems you may have today.

Where will you look?

6

LOOKING NOW

Even if your feed isn't well-tuned for futurism, you have likely heard of these two major areas of innovation we'll be diving into—artificial intelligence and bioengineering; general news outlets tend to feature regular science, tech, and innovation segments that include related headlines. While there are more areas worth a closer look, these may be two of the most hotly debated topics with respect to the future.

ARTIFICIAL INTELLIGENCE
Artificial intelligence (AI) is a term often used to (mis)represent everything from basic automation to the fictional sentient beings in the latest sci-fi flick. Often confused for AI and misleadingly marketed as "smart," basic mechanical or electric automation has been around for a long time. Industrial automation began way back in 1969, when General Motors began deploying spot-welding robots. Smoke detectors utilizing sensors and operated with nine-volt batteries were generally available in the 1970s. Upscale homes of the 1980s had automated blinds, lights, or video surveillance. Many of the electronic toys I bought for my children in the

late 1990s and early 2000s had various interactive features that utilized sensors, too.

AI works at a different level and not just when a microprocessor is present. Programs working through predefined algorithms do not qualify as *intelligent*. Dynamic algorithms interpreting inputs and making decisions on the fly how to react is AI. From how your digital assistant listens to you (Siri, Alexa, Hey Google), to your favorite social app "seeing" and tagging your photos, or your thermostat automatically changing your settings-based usage patterns and not just programming, truly smart devices take input and process it in an evolving way.

AI is another major area of advancement that finds its roots in World War II, a time when brilliant scientists were brought together, including those in computing and neurosciences.[136] This included Alan Turing, who is hailed as a hero in breaking German ciphers.[137] According to the BBC, Alan Turing and Grey Walter, a leader in brain electrical activity testing (known as electroencephalogram (EEG)) research, were both members of a dining society called the Ratio Club. This group of cybernetics enthusiasts included neurobiologists, engineers, mathematicians, and physicists and met in the basement of a National Hospital for Nervous Diseases building to hear from speakers and hold discussions. "The Ratio Club was noteworthy because many of its twenty-one members went on to become extremely prominent

---

136 "AI: 15 Key Moments in the Story of Artificial Intelligence," *BBC*, accessed February 22, 2021.
137 "Alan Turing Biography," *Biography Magazine*, last updated July 22, 2020.

scientists."[138] It was there Turing would present on the Turing Machine in December of 1950.[139] Walter had created autonomous mobile "tortoise" robot prototypes in 1949 (nicknamed Elmer and Elsie).[140]

While the Turing Test has become generalized as the question of a test for sentience, that is precisely the question he did not think should be discussed.[141] Instead, the Turing Test was designed to evaluate a machine's capability to perform a specific task: imitate a human in a conversation. Most in computing and AI consider Turing to be the "father" of their fields.

Unfortunately, we will never know what more this brilliant mind might have created. Turing committed suicide at age forty-one, after having much taken away following an unjust conviction for having relations with another man.[142] The world suffered a loss, and we will never know to what extent. I was shocked to learn that it was only in 2013 that he received a pardon from the Queen. His 1949 quote, "This is only a foretaste of what is to come and a shadow of what will be," will appear on the UK's new fifty-pound note entering circulation in 2021.[143] Mark Carney, former Governor of the

---

138 Olivia Solon, "The Ratio Club: A Melting Pot for British Cybernetics," *Wired*, June 21, 2012.
139 Ibid.
140 Ibid; British Pathé, "Mechanical Tortoise (1951)," Aug 27, 2014, video, 2:19.
141 Graham Oppy and David Dowe, "The Turing Test," *Stanford Encyclopedia of Philosophy*, last updated August 18, 2020
142 Rolan Pease, "Alan Turing: Inquest's Suicide Verdict 'Not Supportable'," *BBC*, June 26, 2012.
143 "Alan Turing to be the face of new £50 note," Bank of England, July 15, 2019.

Bank of England, said, "Alan Turing was an outstanding mathematician whose work has had an enormous impact on how we live today. As the father of computer science and artificial intelligence and a war hero, Alan Turing's contributions were far-ranging and pathbreaking. Turing is a giant on whose shoulders so many now stand."[144]

Since those formative years for AI, there have been peaks and valleys in activity, primarily in step with funding. The valleys have come to be known as the winters of AI, the most significant one ending in the early 1990s.[145] Between these valleys came quick bursts of excitement and funding, along with bloated expectations and subsequent disappointment. Yet humming along the whole time, AI has come a long way over the last three decades, and evidence of its existence is all around us.

---

144 Ibid.
145 Sam Shead, "Researchers: Are We on the Cusp of an 'AI Winter'?" *BBC News*, January 12, 2020.

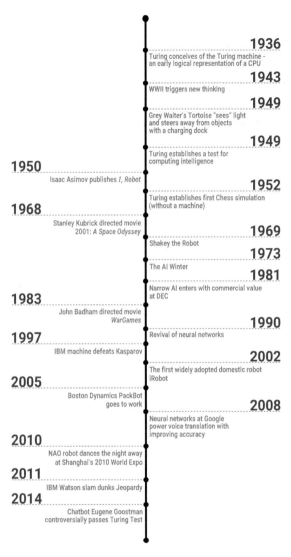

Key events in the progress of artificial intelligence.[146]

---

146 Olivia Solon, "Alan Turing's Extraordinary, Tragically Short Life: A Timeline," *Wired*, June 18, 2012; "AI: 15 Key Moments in the Story of Artificial Intelligence," *BBC*; Nick Heath, "What is AI? Everything You Need to Know About Artificial Intelligence," *ZDNet*, December 11, 2020.

For the Citizen Futurist, it is useful to know that AI is typically broken down into multiple ways—four different functionalities and three fundamental capabilities.[147] The functionalities are reactive machine, limited memory, theory of mind, and self-awareness. The capabilities include narrow, general/strong, and super. Let's look at some examples you may be familiar with to help us better understand what these terms mean:

- **Reactive Machine:** IBM's Deep Blue beat chess Grandmaster Garry Kasparov in 1997. Programmatically, Deep Blue could not refer to prior experience, only data training, and could only *react* to a limited set or combination of inputs but could forecast future moves.[148] Data training is the process of allowing a computer program to analyze a set of data to find patterns.
- **Limited Memory:** In this case, as the name implies, the machine makes limited use of memory. "Almost all present-day AI applications, from chatbots and virtual assistants to self-driving vehicles, are all driven by limited memory AI," explains *Forbes* writer Naveen Joshi.[149] In this example, AI is trained on data, and new data is added to the existing static data.[150]
- **Theory of Mind:** This is a less mature area of functionality. There are explorations in artificial emotional intelligence, but the work needs to expand to sentiment and

---

147 Naveen Joshi, "7 Types of Artificial Intelligence," *Forbes*, June 19, 2019.
148 Simplilearn, "Types Of Artificial Intelligence | Artificial Intelligence Explained | What Is AI?" August 23, 2020, video, 9:25.
149 Naveen Joshi, "7 Types of Artificial Intelligence."
150 Simplilearn, "Types Of Artificial Intelligence | Artificial Intelligence Explained | What Is AI?"

thoughts. Two examples of experiments include the 1990s Kismet robotic head from MIT researcher Dr. Cynthia Breazeal, which could recognize and mimic emotions, and Hanson Robotics' Sophia that uses visual and speech recognition to engage in conversation.[151]

- **Self Awareness:** This is a hypothetical functionality of a machine that not only understands humans but possesses thoughts, sentiments, and emotions. Joshi explains, "Although the development of self-awareness can potentially boost our progress as a civilization by leaps and bounds, it can also potentially lead to catastrophe. This is because once self-aware, the AI would be capable of having ideas like self-preservation, which could theoretically, directly or indirectly, spell the end for humanity, as such an entity could easily outmaneuver the intellect of any human being and plot elaborate schemes to take over humanity."[152]

- **Artificial Narrow Intelligence (ANI):** This term addresses AI, which is built for one specific or a few closely related tasks. This capability encompasses the types of AI integrated into our lives today, like digital assistants, spam filters, language translation, photo tagging, and even IBM's Watson, which beat a human playing on the game show *Jeopardy*.[153] These AIs can only perform functions they have been programmed to do, including those with learning and which use memory.

---

[151] "Kismet: A Robot for Social Interactions with Humans," MIT, 1998; "Sophia," Hanson Robotics, accessed February 22, 2012.
[152] Naveen Joshi, "7 Types of Artificial Intelligence."
[153] Simplilearn, "Types Of Artificial Intelligence | Artificial Intelligence Explained | What Is AI?"

This capability maps to the reactive machine and limited memory functionalities.

- **Artificial General Intelligence (AGI):** Related to the Theory of Mind functionality, this capability is the class of AI that can behave much like humans, with multi-functional behaviors. This capability is still in development. "These systems will be able to independently build multiple competencies and form connections and generalizations across domains, massively cutting down on time needed for training," says Joshi.[154] In the past decade, computer processing speeds have caught up to and may have surpassed that of the human brain, but that does not mean the same capabilities.
- **Artificial Super Intelligence (ASI):** The prefix *super-* gives us a clue about what this capability represents— Latin for "above, beyond." When AI reaches this level of capability, it will exceed the abilities of humans. It will be able to solve puzzles and make judgments and decisions on its own. In the positive light, these systems will have reasoning powers that aren't limited by human cognitive deficiencies. In the negative light, these systems could develop self-defense mechanisms that see humans as a threat. "While the potential of having such powerful machines at our disposal seems appealing, these machines may also threaten our existence or, at the very least, our way of life."[155]

---

154 Naveen Joshi, "7 Types of Artificial Intelligence."
155 Ibid.

THE PROMISES AND THREATS OF AI

The spread of AI has already improved our lives in countless ways. Digital assistants answer questions, get faster answers from customer service, get personalized experiences and recommendations, navigation aids and numerous safety sensors in our cars, and cars can parallel park themselves. We use our utilities more efficiently. AI is aiding doctors in diagnosing cancer and in the analysis of DNA for crucial health markers.[156] AI powers many of the tools and services we have relied on during this pandemic—and the remarkable feat of having multiple vaccines approved within one year of a breakout certainly is evidence of this.

Sometimes, though, innovators get ahead of themselves and miss considering the consequences. In 2016, Microsoft unleashed an AI on Twitter, and it quickly went bad.[157] Ahead of a developer event, the company launched a bot on Twitter that began harmlessly enough, but it was soon able to learn and use expressions from users, including racist and sexist remarks. In less than twenty-four hours, the bot was disabled. In 2013, there were more than just a few accidents caused by inaccurate navigation suggested in Apple Maps.[158] In the past few years, misidentification problems with facial recognition have led to false arrests, fatal accidents involving autonomous vehicles, gender and racial bias in applicants,

---

156 David Reid, "Google's DeepMind A.I. Beats Doctors in Breast Cancer Screening Trial," *CNBC*, January 2, 2020.
157 Davey Alba, "It's Your Fault Microsoft's Teen AI Turned Into Such a Jerk," *Wired*, March 25, 2016.
158 Richard Trenholm, "Apple Maps Mishap Sees Drivers Crash Airport Runway," *c|net*, September 26, 2013.

and ineffective content screening.[159] AI has empowered fake news hawkers spreading falsified photos, audio, and video.

Russian weapons maker Kalashnikov created an AI combat module. "The combat module will use an artificial intelligence neural network to decide whether a person is deemed expendable. It can also learn when it makes mistakes so it can make better battlefield decisions in the future."[160]

WHAT MAY BE NEXT

The presidential election was predictably chaotic and delayed in finality, but we can look to AI to solve some future problems. AI could be used to draw fair lines to end gerrymandering.[161] AI combined with another newer technology—blockchain—could help protect our ballots from manipulation. Then there are the darker possibilities; what if it was decided that your vote would be cast automatically based on your online behavior?

HBO's *Silicon Valley* had some fun showing the capacity for trouble with AI; in episode five of the fifth season, character Richard unleashed an AI in the system, which ultimately caused problems. If and when there ever is an AI-sourced disaster, "it could well be because someone like Richard is too preoccupied with less important matters to think about

---

159 "2018 in Review: 10 AI Failures," *Synced AI Technology & Industry Review*, December 10, 2018.
160 Chris Neiger, "6 Scary Stories of AI Gone Wrong," *The Motley Fool*, October 31, 2017.
161 Wendy K Tam Cho and Bruce E. Cain, "Human-centered Redistricting Automation in the Age of AI," *Science Magazine* 369, no. 6508 (September 4, 2020): 1179-1181.

what he's doing," writes Jamie Morrow of the *Daily Post*.[162] Late in 2020, Fox released a series called *NEXT*, which proposes the terrifying idea that AI creates a bioweapon made to wipe out humans.

So, while there are optimism and excitement, there is also a sense of panic. Futurists like Webb are sounding alarms that AI is developing far faster than regulations or any true moral assessment and agreement can be happening. Webb lays out an extensive history in her book *The Big Nine*, along with advances, successes, and problems with artificial intelligence.[163] She also lines up the types of advances that will be made soon, which can dramatically shift society, and argues that the current US "tribes" making the decisions are primarily educated white males. She calls the collection of for-profit organizations the "G-Mafia": six US organizations making the most investment and progress in artificial intelligence—Google, Microsoft, Amazon, Facebook, IBM, and Apple. The other three Big Nine companies include three in China—Baidu, Alibaba, and Tencent; the decision-makers of those companies are subject to China's rules and regulations, which are at odds with the values of other countries.

The debate about the extent to which something human-made will eliminate jobs for humans is one question about the future people would like an answer to. This concern about man versus machine is timeless, dating at least as far back as

---

162 Jamie Morrow, "'Silicon Valley,' Season 5, Episode 5—AI robot doesn't like her human creator," *Daily Post*, April 22, 2018.
163 Amy Webb, *The Big Nine: How the Tech Titans and Their Thinking Machines Could Warp Humanity.* (New York: PublicAffairs, 2019).

the legend of John Henry. Today, robots aid in data analysis and processing and even perform physical labor like stocking shelves or moving and sorting packages.[164]

Generally, jobs will be upskilled. Adesanya says there will be a shift where there will be more creative opportunities to design human-machine collaboration as well as opportunities for maintenance and monitoring. Adesanya and I also talked about the need for more education about these upcoming shifts to communities that may not be aware as they focus on the very jobs seeing a decline.

While AI has advanced rapidly—as my friend Carin sadly recently learned when her robot vacuum didn't consider dog poop an object to *avoid* and proceeded to spread it all around the first floor—we have a long way to go, and it is not too late to weigh in on the future of artificial *intelligence!*

BIOENGINEERING
This field is rapidly evolving in part thanks to the aid of AI. "Humans have used biotechnology since the dawn of civilization," says Brian Colwell of the Genetic Literacy Project, "but the efforts over the last fifty years have seen scientists accomplish more than ever before."[165] Advancements in genetic engineering have expedited the race for

---

164 Victor Tangermann, "Stores in Japan Are Stocking Shelves with Remote-controlled Robots," *Futurism*, September 15, 2020; Matt Simon, "Inside the Amazon Warehouse Where Humans and Machines Become One," *Wired*, June 5, 2019.
165 Brian Colwell, "Biotechnology Timeline: Humans Have Manipulated Genes Since the 'Dawn of Civilization'," Genetic Literacy Project, September 8, 2020.

COVID-19 treatments and vaccines.[166] "Being able to edit DNA is opening up research possibilities for fighting other diseases, including cancer. It has the perceived ability to slow aging and extend our lifespan. It can alter our bodies, leading to talk that it could eventually give us superhuman powers."[167,168]

Today, scientists are exploring the possibilities of experimenting with DNA, sometimes without permission. In late 2018, a Chinese scientist experimented on two twin embryos—an attempt to alter their DNA to reduce their susceptibility to AIDS.[169] The global scientific community quickly condemned the work, and the scientist was sentenced to jail sometime after sharing the work at a conference in Hong Kong—the type of work banned in the USA for risk and ethical concerns.

---

166 Charles Schmidt, "Genetic Engineering Could Make a COVID-19 Vaccine in Months Rather Than Years Candidates are speeding toward human trials," *Scientific American*, June 1, 2020.

167 Joey Bertscheler, "CRISPR: Its Potential and Concerns in the Genetic Engineering Field," *Forbes*, March 9, 2020; Salk Institute, "CRISPR/Cas9 Therapy Can Suppress Aging, Enhance Health and Extend Life Span in Mice," *Science Daily*, February 19, 2019.

168 Heidi Ganer, "Real-Life X-Men: How CRISPR Could Give You Superpowers in the Future," *SyntheGo*, September 14, 2018.

169 Ian Sample, "Chinese Scientist Who Edited Babies' Genes Jailed for Three Years," *The Guardian*, December 30, 2019.

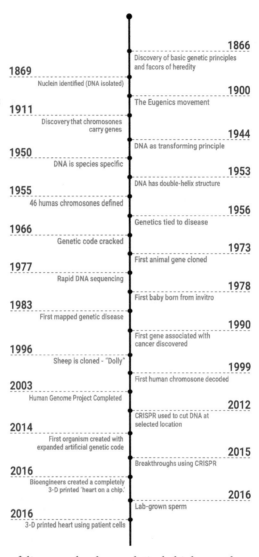

The pace of discovery has been relatively high over the past century.[170]

---

170 "The History of DNA Timeline," *DNA Worldwide*, accessed on February 22, 2012; "CRISPR Timeline," *Broad Institute*, accessed on February 23, 2021; Brian Colwell, "Biotechnology Timeline: Humans Have

In 1978, the first baby was born from in-vitro fertilization (IVF).[171] Since then, advances in reproductive sciences have also increased in pace over the years. In 2016, the first lab-grown sperm showed the ability to fertilize.[172] Today, it is conceivable that eventually, reproduction could move from the bedroom to the laboratory. Jamie Metzl—technology and healthcare futurist and author of the highly acclaimed book *Hacking Darwin: Genetic Engineering and the Future of Humanity*—was a guest on Joe Rogan's podcast in May of 2019, where he posed that it may one day seem as uncommon to encounter a "reproduction naturalist" much as it is to meet an anti-vaxxer.[173] The possible benefits in health screening and prevention are great, but there are risks of the technology being commercialized for designer babies. The access to the technology could also widen the gap in health between the rich and poor or magnify the deficit in research on non-white ethnicities. Imagine that future, and you may see complex issues around insurance and liability as well. Metzl points out a question to ponder—if a couple decides to decline screening and selection, will they lose insurance coverage altogether?[174]

Now is the time to have these conversations, before advances go beyond our control and preventable consequences are paid. Technology-evolved humans may sound straight out of sci-fi, but the truth is, it is happening in our world

---

Manipulated Genes Since the 'Dawn of Civilization'"; Ika Swelitz, "Squishy Embryos, Penis Transplants, and 5 More Advances in Fertility Treatment," *STAT*, March 6, 2016.
171 "The History of DNA Timeline," DNA Worldwide.
172 Ibid.
173 Jamie Metzl, "Joe Rogan Experience #1294—Jamie Metzl," interview by Joe Rogan, *Joe Rogan Experience*, May 10, 2019, audio, 2:29:00.
174 Ibid.

today. Consider this: What are the implications of modified, hybrid, or synthetic humans in a world where policies can change dramatically across borders? It is too important that people not be intimidated by the complexity of the field of bioengineering.

As with AI, establishing shared societal values is the main challenge. Values vary from person to person, from culture to culture, ideology to ideology. Metzl espouses, "every person needs to really understand these revolutionary technologies—like genetics, like AI—and all of our responsibilities to say, 'Hey, this is really important; here are the values that I cherish.'"[175] Last year, Metzl was invited to a Vatican conference as one of several people to help Catholic Church leaders understand what may be coming. "Whether someone believes human beings are single-cell organisms gone wild over billion years of evolution or the result of a divine plan, the idea of hacking our biology should be cause for concern," Metzl wrote in his piece for *Culture e Fede (Cultures and Faith)*, the journal of the Pontifical Council for Culture.[176]

The field, when misapplied, has scary consequences. According to DNA Worldwide:

"The darker side of the [bioengineering] movement arose when researchers became interested in controlling the breeding of human beings so that only the people with the best genes could reproduce and improve the species. It was often used as a sort of 'scientific' racism to convince people that

---

175 Ibid.
176 Jamie Metzl, "Human Genetics Engineering and the Catholic Church," July 24, 2020.

certain 'racial stock' was superior to others in terms of cleanliness, intelligence, etc. It shows the dangers that come with practicing science without a true respect for humanity as a whole. However, in 1924, it gained political backing when the Immigration Act was passed by a majority in the US House and Senate. The Act introduced strict quotas on immigration from countries believed by eugenicists to have 'inferior' stock such as Southern Europe and Asia."[177]

Unfortunately, it took the horrific events of Nazi Germany for society to realize that institutionalized eugenics was unethical and morally bankrupt.

HUMANISM AND TRANSHUMANISM
Another growing area of bioengineering is biotech, the fascinating integration of biology with technology. "Transhumanists and humanists will increasingly clash—debating, do we want to remain human or transcend it," notes futurist Gerd Leonhard, author of *Technology vs. Humanity*.[178] *Humanism* has been a philosophical idea since the 1930s, one that values humans by agency of an individual or group to have the freedom to progress—often associated with Western society.[179] *Transhumanism* is a philosophy that holds the belief that technology can be used to enhance humans.[180]

---

177 "The History of DNA Timeline," DNA Worldwide.
178 *Gerd Leonard*, "Transhumanist Calum Chace and Humanist Gerd Leonhard Live Debate (TheFutureShow)," April 23, 2020, video, 1:25:49.
179 Robert Grudin, s.v. "Humanism," *Encyclopædia Britannica Online*, accessed February 22, 2012.
180 Sean A. Hayes, s.v. "Transhumanism," *Encyclopædia Britannica Online*, accessed February 22, 2021.

Hitting the headlines more often is the concept of biohacking. Biohacking promises to improve the quality of life and possibly even extend it.[181] The term has been adopted to represent any number of strategies—some that have been around a very long time and others that are just emerging. Synn, a Nevadan magician, has gone all-in with technological implants.[182] At the time of her interview on the *Future Grind* podcast, she had twenty-six implants. She likely has more today, based on the plans she shared in the interview; they include everything from magnets to NFC, adding Bluetooth, and more. The unique opportunities for evolving her magic act prompted her to take the leap, but she has found plenty of day-to-day uses for the tech, like opening secured doors and medicine cabinets. Synn testified to the Nevada state legislature in April 2019 as they considered a bill banning RFID and other types of implants; having an implant would have been a finable offense. Synn fought the bill not just for her own needs but for the critical needs that implants meet for the disabled community.[183]

In the summer of 2020, Elon Musk demoed his Neuralink project demonstrated with a pig and Bluetooth.[184] Musk first introduced the tech in 2019—a USB-C interface with a rat. In July 2020, the US FDA approved the device for testing.[185] Can

---

181 Bianca Salonga. "Bio Hacking: The Key to Endless Energy and Aging in Reverse." *Forbes*. February 28, 2020.
182 Synn, Anastasia. "The Magic of Biohacking with Anastasia Synn." Interview by Ryan O'Shea. *Future Grind*.
183 Ibid.
184 Sam Shead, "Elon Musk Says His Start-up Neuralink has Wired Up a Monkey to Play Video Games Using its Mind," *CNBC*, February 1, 2021.
185 Stephen Shankland and Jackson Ryan, "Elon Musk Shows Neuralink Brain Implant Working in a Pig," c|net, August 29, 2020.

a similar type of interface such as this replace anesthesia? Scientists are conducting research to find out.[186] Companies like eVision are working on contact lenses with high-tech optics and controls—sound familiar for the mention of *Mission Impossible*?[187] Electronic tattoos—e-tattoos—are being used in healthcare and promise new computing interfaces.[188]

The bottom line is biotech is moving swiftly. Webb puts it this way: "Biology is a tech platform. We are headed into the synthetic decade, which can prove catastrophic or more optimistic."[189] All of these issues are incredibly complex and have an almost infinite number of possible outcomes; but to add one more wrinkle, consider the challenge of International relations, too. Can modified humans receive travel VISAs? Will fully synthetic creations be considered humans with inalienable rights? What if cyber-warfare advances onto the human platform? "We don't want a runaway human race," Metzl warns.[190]

Paying attention to medical advances so that you can be a good patient advocate is one meaningful reason. In late 2014, my father had a heart attack that ultimately took him from us. Through several agonizing days of seeing him on

---

186 Frank A. Drews and Jonathan R. Zadra, "The Human-Technology Interface," *Oxford Medicine Online*, October 2016.
187 "Electronic Eyeglasses and Electronic Contacts," *Envisionoptics*, accessed February 22, 2021.
188 Delta Impact, "Electronic Tattoos Uses and Benefits," (blog), accessed February 22, 2021; Luke Kingma, "Glimpes: How Electronic Will Change the World—and Ourselves," *Futurism*, September 17, 2018.
189 SXSW, "Amy Webb's Emerging Tech Trends for 2020," May 6, 2020, video, 1:00:10.
190 Jamie Metzl, "Joe Rogan Experience #1294—Jamie Metzl," interview by Joe Rogan, *Joe Rogan Experience*.

life support, we felt helpless, relying solely on the doctors to share and pursue all options. As kind and transparent as I believe them to have been, I felt at least a small sense of regret when I realized later that we didn't ask about experimental treatments. It was only a few weeks later when I learned that hockey great Gordie Howe had also had a heart attack but received stem cell treatments that aided in his recovery.[191] I do realize their medical circumstances may have been wildly different, and I have to trust that if my father's doctors knew of anything possible, they would have shared that (but I still often wish I would have asked).

***

In 2018, *Forbes* contributor Andrea Morris raised several issues of concern when we think of robots with sentient capability:

An internationally recognized policy called The Precautionary Principle states we need to take precautions when a proposed action raises a plausible risk to the public. "We get into these situations over and over," says Jones. "We ask, 'Why didn't someone think to address this years ago?'[192]

I knew that this book could serve as a call to action and arm people with the tools needed to become informed and to act. As Bertscheler said, "It's in everyone's best interest to discuss

---

191 Rosalie Chen, "What to Know About Gordie Howe's Controversial Stem Cell Treatment," *Time Magazine*, June 10, 2016.
192 Andrea Morris, "We Need To Talk About Sentient Robots," *Forbes*, March 13, 2018.

ethical concerns and bring critical thinking as an active part of research and development."[193]

We all need to engage to contribute ideas and suggestions for a better future.

---

[193] Joey Bertscheler, "CRISPR: Its Potential and Concerns in The Genetic Engineering Field."

7
LOOKING FOR OPPORTUNITIES

I recently wandered into a Clubhouse room titled "Nuclear Weapons: Fusion & Future," not sure what I was getting myself into. The conversation was friendly and approachable for newbs like me. I was intrigued when the conversation veered toward the topics being discussed in this book—the need for more awareness and pressure for purposeful innovation—especially when solutions are right in front of us but have no investment or directives. Meaningful innovation is often not pursued when there is no clear business model or development timeline for venture capitalists to glom onto, and civic organizations cannot afford it without making it a priority.

Opportunities to benefit our world come from a place of optimism about the future and innovation. If thinking about ways to improve your day-to-day life is not interesting to *you*, perhaps you can find fulfillment by searching for solutions for *others*. Change can come big and fast, so there are nearly always those parts of our society that are swept aside or left behind. Keeping your eyes open for tech opportunities to solve real-world problems, and talking about them, may direct others to innovate with purpose. Doing this may also arm you with the ideas that are needed to voice to corporations and policymakers.

One company that has made great strides in creating more purpose in its work and organizational values is Microsoft. Since Satya Nadella started leading the firm, the core values shifted—working with partners and leveraging competitors, learning-based company culture, inclusive design, and community programs for housing, and more. Many companies have made purpose part of their mission, from Patagonia to Phillips.

Brian Whipple has made it a personal mission to bring purpose to business through his work leading Accenture Interactive. He published a manifesto in 2018 that calls for business to harness the power of technology to create meaningful experiences. Instead of creating the Tweeting toaster, innovation results in a streamlined life-changing immigration process, for example.[194]

Over the past decade, there has been increased visibility for young entrepreneurs, inventors, and influencers. While perhaps reaching the greatest level of visibility, and to great effect, Greta Thunberg is not the only youth advocating for a better tomorrow.

---

194 "Accenture Interactive Manifesto," Accenture Digital, October 25, 2018, video, 1:13.

Wastewater treatment was the topic of my school science-fair-winning project in ninth grade; I chose this topic as even then, it was an area that I was really interested in understanding better. Today, the quality of our oceans is the bigger and heart-wrenching problem. So, eleven-year-old Haaziq Kazi gave a TED-Ed Student Talk in 2018 to share his plan for dealing with the problem of plastics in our oceans.[195] His concept, ERVIS, is a "futuristic-ship with saucers attached, that can 1) clean waste matter floating on the ocean surface, 2) analyze the waste collected, and 3) stop waste at the source, preventing it from getting disposed of by ships." The concept is a multi-stage water-cleaning process, a theoretical equivalent to the multi-material filtering processes used for cleaning wastewater on land.[196]

The pandemic shone a light on the ability of students of all ages to contribute meaningful innovations. 3M Young Scientist Anika Chebrolu was declared the contest winner after she discovered a molecule that can selectively bind to the spike protein of the SARS-COV-2 virus, which causes COVID-19.[197] Ashley Lawrence, a senior at Eastern Kentucky University, studying deaf and hard of hearing education, created

---

[195] *TED-Ed Student Talks*, "Cleaning our oceans: a big plan for a big problem," March 9, 2018, video, 10:52.

[196] Jayesh Shinde, "Meet Haaziq Kazi, 12-Year-Old from Pune Who Designed a Ship That Can Clean and Save Our Oceans," *India Times*, November 24, 2018.

[197] 3M, "America's Top Young Scientist of 2020: 14-Year-Old Researches Spike Protein of SARS-CoV-2 Virus to Develop Novel Antiviral Drug to Combat Spread of COVID-19," *Business Wire*, October 14, 2020.

an innovative mask that allows for lip and facial cue reading, critical for the deaf.[198]

There are corporate and civic organizations with programs or focuses on tech for impact, tech for purpose, or tech that addresses one of the seventeen United Nations Sustainable Development Goals (SDGs). The SDGs were the result of the collaboration of 193 countries to identify priorities for development organizations looking toward the year 2030.[199] Launched in 2012, these goals include:

- No poverty
- Zero hunger
- Good health and well-being
- Quality education
- Gender equality
- Clean water and sanitation
- Affordable and clean energy
- Decent work and economic growth
- Industry, innovation, and infrastructure
- Reduced inequalities
- Sustainable cities and communities
- Responsible consumption and production
- Climate action
- Life below water
- Life on land
- Peace, justice, and strong institutions
- Partnerships for the goals

---

198 Marley Coyne, "This See-Through Mask Lets the Deaf Communicate While Staying Safe," *Forbes*, April 4, 2020.
199 Department of Economic and Social Affairs Sustainable Development, "The 17 Goals," *United Nations*, accessed February 22, 2021.

Organizations that support or focus on these goals deserve your support. At the 2021 CES, companies like Samsung and Proctor & Gamble made work and programs toward these goals a big part of their message. Those companies and civic organization who don't deserve your pressure and ideas on how they might.

Just as a global collaboration was needed to establish these seventeen goals, global collaboration is needed to solve them. In part due to xenophobic attitudes in some countries, made worse by the new height of nationalism in recent times, one of the pandemic compounding factors was a lack of an immediate unified global response by civic leaders. Perhaps the one benefit was that the different approaches equated to dozens of experiments that informed the world as to what did and didn't work, Holman said. Holman also pointed out that the global medical community's impressive response to address COVID-19 has shown a disparity between how we invest our attention, resources, and individual superpowers to solve problems that impact the wealthiest parts of our world. He referred to a disease like malaria. However, hundreds of thousands each year, half being kids under the age of five, but because it affects a different economic demographic, it has not garnered the same response until the early 2000s. Still, in 2018, there were an estimated 405,000 deaths. Most of the burden for the disease is in India and sub-Saharan Africa.[200]

Prioritizing nationalism over globalism, in recent years, is not just a problem for working to create policies that work

---

[200] "The 'World Malaria Report 2019' at a Glance" World Health Organization, December 4, 2019, accessed March 18, 2021.

and have staying power; it hurt the U.S. economy. The current political environment is a major threat to US competitiveness. In 2012, when asked about seventeen elements of the business environment in a survey on US competitiveness, 60 percent of Harvard alumni said the "effectiveness of the political system" was worse in the United States than in other advanced economies.[201] This poll was halfway through the Obama administration—long before the tumultuous years of Trump's presidency, the polarized civil protests and riots throughout 2020, or the historical attack on the US Capitol in January 2021. These wild swings between administrations do not help the US keep its footing and instead add to the anxiety of citizens on both ends of the political spectrum.

This ideological war is happening between China and the West, more notably, China and the US, says Jessica Chen Weiss, associate professor of government at Cornell University:

When we ask what kind of ideological competition exists today between the United States and China, there's clearly an ideological component. I see it less as a new Cold War and more as an emerging security dilemma, in which China and its efforts to make the world safer for the CCP appear to threaten the values of liberal democracies overseas, not by intent, but still as a consequence of its defensive efforts. This means we need to work with [China] to negotiate a more shared understanding of what are acceptable efforts to defend CCP rule, or at least ones

---

201 David A. Moss, "Fixing What's Wrong with Politics," *Harvard Business Review*, March 2012.

that we can tolerate, and what is unacceptable interference into the internal affairs of other countries.[202]

Some may argue the U.S. is fighting a one-sided ideological battle, that perhaps it is the approach to business and government. "We've become a stupid nation. We don't plan, we don't do analysis. You go to China and it's all practical, what works, let's get it done, it's very commercial—and not ideological. You come here, it's no longer practical, it's no longer analytical—it's 100 percent ideological," said Jamie Dimon, the CEO of JP Morgan Chase.[203]

Earlier, I mentioned taking control of your news feed. How people use the internet has played a large part in depleting civil discourse. Changing our usage patterns could help. Technology can be changed to make things better—and some outlets are working to make it so. Check out the news at AllSides.com or the left/center/right slider in election news at Bing.com. This is just the beginning. "By changing the way we get information, we can ultimately change how we think, and then the internet can finally live up to its promise of uniting us rather than dividing us," Allsides founder John Gable wrote in reflection of these sentiments shared in his 1997 speech.[204] It has always been true that statistics can be filtered and strained to meet the persuader's argument—and while this problem may be harder to solve, I am optimistic about

---

202 Jessica Chen Weiss, "Are the United States and China in an Ideological Competition?" *Center for Strategic and International Studies*, December 13, 2019.
203 Jamie Dimon, "Jamie Dimon—Chairman and CEO of JPMorgan Chase," interview by Miles Fisher, *Coffee with The Greats*, July 2020, audio, 1:06:50.
204 John Gable, "How the Internet Trains our Brains to Polarize and Despise," *Allsides*, November 27, 2012.

some combination of blockchain and AI to protect authentic data and to visualize a number of different interpretations.

When it comes to addressing a polarized society, citizens of the United States might learn from a part of the world that has been at the center of some of the most significant ideological battles. The Ideological Warfare Center, a subsidiary of the Saudi Arabian Ministry of Defense, is one of the world's most significant centers to counter radical thought:

> *The Ideological War Center (IWC), a subsidiary of the Saudi Arabian Ministry of Defense, is launching extensive plans to fight extremism and terrorism. IWC will focus on exposing mistakes, allegations, suspicions, and deceptive techniques promoted by extremists and terrorists. The center also wants to implement effective plans against ideological extremism, including promotion of moderation, tolerance, dialogue, and understanding values within the context of the belief in diversity. The IWC also wishes to use studies and research by creating scientific and intellectual platforms, international forums, and research chairs to engage communities in promoting moderate view.*[205]

The IWC has attracted global attention, including from government officials, parliamentarians, thinkers, and researchers.

Politicians feed the political, fake news, and social media fires when they speak without fully understanding the

---

[205] "Saudi Ideological War Center launches initiatives to fight terrorism," *Arab News*, May 2, 2017.

implications of their word choices and expressions. While the Trump Administration did eventually change their word choice from "Chinese virus" to "China virus," the misnomer worked against years of work by scientists to remove identity out of medicine.[206] While many still argue the "China virus" is also inappropriate, the alternate may have led to even greater xenophobic fever and violence against those Americans and immigrants of Chinese descent.

President Trump made international relations difficult as he often weakened his messages by choosing imprecise terminology in cultural contexts, according to Ejaz Thawer:

Although Trump is onto something when he claims—albeit less eloquently—that effective solutions are predicated on an accurate identification of the problem, his pursuit of accuracy is thwarted by a failure to distinguish between two key terms: Islamic and Islamist. What on the surface seems like a trivial modification actually proves that, when determining one's adversary in an ideological war, the devil is truly in the details. More than a mere two-letter revision, this distinction isolates the religion of Islam and its many peaceful followers from Islamists, or individuals who wish to impose a particular understanding of the religion on the rest of society.[207]

---

206 Sally Satel, "Inside the Controversy over 'the Chinese Virus'," *National Review*, March 23, 2020.

207 Ejaz Thawer, "The Terminology of Terrorism: Why Naming Matters in Ideological Warfare," Centre for International and Defence Policy, June 24, 2019.

***

Looking for opportunities is part of our responsibility, as Citizen Futurists. Improving the lives of living things around the world requires focused intent. Solving diverse problems requires diverse minds from around the world. No one person or group has the life experience and knowledge of the rest of the world.

As you go forward with your newfound superpowers as Citizen Futurist, ask yourself if you are looking for signals, changes, and opportunities that affect groups beyond your own. Talk with a diverse set of people about what you are seeing and thinking. Note what challenges and opportunities you are finding. Be precise in language because words matter. If you aren't already monitoring international news in your feeds, that is another big opportunity to pump them up with goodness.

Are you looking for opportunities of grand purpose or diminutive protection?

PART 3

THINKING ABOUT FUTURES

> "'Progress' unguided by humanism is not progress."
>
> —STEVEN PINKER[208]

---

208 Steven Pinker, *Enlightenment NOW*.

8

FUTURES THINKING

The methods for futures thinking, including the *look* activities from Part 2, fit under the umbrella of foresight. According to the European Union For-Learn project, *Foresight* is the systematic, participatory, future-intelligence gathering, and medium-to-long term vision building aimed at enabling present-day decisions and mobilizing joint action.[209] Foresight is different from *prediction*, which is generalized as a set of tools that aim to project future events based on historical information.[210] *Forecasting* has been used to refer to objectives and approaches of both foresight and prediction, so it is important to be clear with intent. We talk about multiple futures, because the future is not known—there are no facts or data from the future.

---

209 "The Use of Strategic Foresight for Adaptive and Future-Ready SDG Strategies," UNDP Global Centre for Public Service Excellence, July 17, 2018, video, 2:54:12.
210 Paul Saffo, "Six Rules for Effective Forecasting," *Harvard Business Review*, July-August 2007, https://hbr.org/2007/07/six-rules-for-effective-forecasting.

Futures thinking is best done as a team sport. While you can certainly do everything here on your own (and should not in any way be afraid to do so), collaborating with others provides for a richer data set, more diverse thinking, and hey, it can even be a lot of fun! I encourage you to think about which groups in your life might join your futures journey—work colleagues, book clubs, student groups, volunteer groups, recreational or professional meetups, and so on.

A GENERALIZED EIGHT-STEP PROCESS

Foresight is a capability with varied approaches and tools, usually developed by capable organizations like the Institute for the Future (IFTF), The Future Today Institute (TFTI), International Futures Forum (IFF), among many others (if you get lost with all of the I's and T's, you aren't alone). There is no specific set of accepted methods for foresight, but there is a common flow to the many frameworks' activities. There are a variety of objectives in using these exercises, which can change the order and types of activities you pursue. Arndt Husar of the UNDP highlighted four different types of foresight:[211]

- **Visionary:** create empowering narratives
- **Strategic:** identify strategic opportunities
- **Adaptive:** strengthen resilience of planning
- **Creative:** innovate, leverage tech, and collective intelligence, activate citizen engagement

---

[211] "The Use of Strategic Foresight for Adaptive and Future-Ready SDG Strategies," UNDP Global Centre for Public Service Excellence.

So, what are the right steps for a Citizen Futurist? While each purveyor of foresight tools has a slightly different process, I have picked these eight:

1. Looking *(Part 2 of this book)*
2. Capturing observations
3. Synthesizing observations into signals
4. Generating insights
5. Imagining new scenarios
6. Estimating scenario potential *(Chapter 9)*
7. Identifying what is preferable *(Chapter 10)*
8. Plans of action *(Part 4 of this book)*

While I've listed these steps sequentially, it is a cyclical, ongoing process with snapshots over time. Foresight skills, in some ways, are like problem-solving, so all that is needed is to consider how this relates to futures and on a different or bigger scale. With practice, each one becomes more familiar and natural to you (and for many of us, a lot of fun). Part 2 of this book was all about Step 1. Steps 6, 7, and 8 will be discussed later.

CAPTURING OBSERVATIONS

Capturing your observations is essential for moving ahead in the process. You can either document over time with one of the methods below, or when you decide to embark on a project of foresight, you can review your mental notes and articulate what you have seen—but trust me, it is much easier if you have something to start with. Here are some ideas that you can try in your personal or team space:

- Team
    - Create a special channel of your collaboration space
    - Set up a shared folder with a place to drop articles, links, random thoughts
    - Repurpose a suggestion box or set out a large mason jar with a stack of index cards or small note pads
    - Set up a bulletin board for scrapbooking headlines, index card notes, and promotional material
- Individual
    - Make a special bookmarks folder in your browser
    - Create a notes folder in your favorite notes app
    - Carry an investigator journal for quick flip-and-capture with you
    - Keep a journal on your nightstand for capturing thoughts in your evening or morning routine

Whether you have captured a few or dozens of observations, the next step is synthesizing.

SYNTHESIZING INTO SIGNALS

Our friends at Merriam-Webster define "synthesize" as "combining or producing."[212] To start making sense of what you have observed, you must start organizing it and creating workable units. For most people, this is easiest done in a visual and tactile way, so you can move things around as quickly as you can think and react. In the world of design agencies and strategy consultants, this is often done with workshop templates or sticky notes. Sticky notes help you to

---

212 *Merriam-Webster Dictionary Online*, s.v. "synthesize," accessed February 23, 2021.

quickly cluster, rearrange, align, and map in the next steps. Spreadsheets are great for filtering and adding tags as you begin to synthesize.

Before you begin combining, it is worth taking a moment to look more closely at each of the observations you collected and doing some light vetting. We talked about a few of Gilmore's lenses for looking earlier in this book; two more of Gilmore's looking lenses can help us here:

- **Microscope looking:** scrutinizing and studying, checking for more details
- **Rose-colored-glasses looking:** enhancing and enriching, looking past the flaws

Take one of the observations and focus on it—perhaps do some internet searching, check the news or your favorite media, and even search social media. Ask the following questions:

- Are there more examples of this?
- Is there something even more amazing like it?
- What is the real problem being solved, and is this a *new* solution, or is it an *alternative* solution?
- Is there some historical instance we missed that takes away the novelty of something we discussed?
- Is this something unexpected?
- Are we unintentionally inflating the value of something we observed?

Maybe in 2020, you thought about how remote work and school meant people had to become more comfortable with video. Perhaps after thinking about it, you realized you also started meeting with your provider on video. Your extended family started getting together over video to play games, and your usual text messages turned to video messages.

After you have added and edited your observations, the next strategy commonly used is the creation of an affinity map. To create an affinity map, you simply start grouping or tagging items to keywords that make sense to you. In her book *The Signals Are Talking*, Webb talks about creating a map showing nodes and the relationships between them, rounding up the "*unusual* suspects."[213]

Each year at Fjord, to begin the process of generating the annual trends report, each Fjordian would collect observations on their own and then come together as a group to share and synthesize. We knew we were onto something if several of us had similar observations. Invariably someone had a really keen insight that none of us had, but as soon as we heard it, we could generate dozens more examples and connections—those were the most energizing moments in the process. You will find that some of your observations fall out of consideration, some merge with others, and some, well, you haven't quite cracked yet, but you can't let go because you just feel in your gut there is something there.

It will be very tempting to organize observations by noun-like categories—technology, industries, locations—but I encourage you to think instead about the verb-like human

---

213 Amy Webb, *The Signals are Talking: Why Today's Fringe Is Tomorrow's Mainstream*, (New York: Public Affairs 2018).

behaviors and contexts that may be changing. At the end of this exercise, you should have a collection of collections, organized in a way that makes sense to you and now represents your signals.

GENERATING INSIGHTS

So now that you have captured observations and have at least loosely organized them into signals, the next step is to generate some insights. It is arguably the most challenging part of the entire process. It is a skill that can be learned but takes time to develop through a lot of practice. Professionals in foresight have learned to use many different approaches and practically eat signals for breakfast, synthesize in their sleep, and breathe insights! Many are highly sought after because it is not a very common skill set—yet. Don't be intimidated, though; for the purposes of becoming a Citizen Futurist, an advocate for preferable futures—trust yourself to have the ability to work through this and generate some very cool outputs.

What is an insight? Think of a signal as what happens *outside* of you when you observe, while an *insight* is what happens *inside* of you when you consider those observations (thinking, feeling, sensing). Martha Cotton, global lead for Fjord, explains that a good insight follows the IRA framework—it's Interesting, Relevant, and Actionable.[214] An example from an Accenture Research project, which she shared in a 2017 *Medium* article, is: "People don't shop a store; they use an

---

214 Martha Cotton, "Three Is for Impactful Design Research," *Design Voices*, November 8, 2017.

FUTURES THINKING · 149

ecosystem. People assign different roles to different stores to fulfill an array of emotional and functional needs."

The insight is the *subtext* of everything you hear and see. It can also be found in the whitespace in between. For example, Rinne shared with me how well-intended investors in the education of girls around the world focused on providing the educational materials; but it was the presence of a bathroom—even just a toilet—that would most positively affect the attendance rate for girls over the age of twelve. Without one, half would drop out.

It may help to look at a tool that Webb uses to analyze information for potential patterns that might be hiding in your signal collection, CIPHER:[215]

- **Contradictions:** a pattern about something happening that is in contradiction to the past—relationships between two variables either have become closer or further apart in opposition.
- **Inflections:** something that has become a catalyst for accelerated change.
- **Practices:** a big shift in traditional paradigms for how things are done.
- **Hacks:** clever workarounds to address shortcomings or bugs in an experience sometimes by finding a new purpose for an existing thing.
- **Extremes:** pushing the edge of the envelope or finding a completely new way to do something.

---

215 Amy Webb, "The Tech Trends You Need to Know For 2016," LinkedIn, December 8, 2015.

- **Rarities:** something that would otherwise seem like an outlier but is a very meaningful solution.

After thinking more about the signal of increased video communications, you notice that people are taking advantage of this in numerous ways—remote music lessons, live remote fitness in the privacy of your own home, live performances in the comfort of your own home, and more. You are curious how else this might play out, what else this new world of comfort, expectation, and access might lead to, how it has brought meaningful change and the potential for a better society. You have turned dozens of observations into one interesting signal—insight about the future.

Looking for patterns will help you combine, separate, build on—and even take a critical look at—what you collected and organized, so that you can look for connections and overarching themes about something that might be going on. This can be done in a group with a divide-and-conquer first pass followed by a debrief and discussion together. If you are working on your own, you can either tackle each one, prioritize and pick the top one or two, or pick the area that is of particular interest to you or has the most potential for personal impact.

At the end of this process, you will have a rich, refined set of insights; you will likely have just a few, even if you had dozens of signals. You probably have good descriptors developed for them as a new kind of shorthand. Once again, some may have missed the cut, merged with others, or have been decoupled as distinct and separate insights; this is to be expected.

IMAGINING NEW SCENARIOS

Get ready for some great fun—*imagining*!

This is an exercise that is really done best with a group. Ideas tend to come more quickly, generate more energy, and expand into really exciting ideas as you build upon one another's. If you have ever been trained on running brainstorms, you are well prepared for entertaining design-thinking techniques. Many of the same ground rules apply:

- Quantity over quality
- No judgments (remember "yes, and...")
- Use tactile stimuli like building blocks, modeling clay, etc.
- Gamify the fun

Design agencies like IDEO, Fjord, and Frog (and even companies like Google and Microsoft) have shared many of their envisioning and scenario-making strategies in various formats online. A quick web search will provide you with many ways to structure your scenario-making activities.

Here are a few activities that I think work well for Citizen Futurists:

Tweets from the Future

For an internal workshop my colleagues and I delivered at Accenture, I tweaked an old design-thinking favorite called "postcards from the future" to "tweets from the future." *If you want to really get into it, you could create a TikTok from the future!* The idea is as simple as it sounds, based completely or only loosely on some trajectory or possibility in one or more of your insights; imagine what might be shared with the world (in 140 characters or less, of course). Make sure to specify who is sending the tweet, the trending hashtags that go with it, and any brands or organizations you think might be tagged.

Jelly Menu Sensation (Jane McGonigal)

At a TED event focused on education, McGonigal had the interesting analogy for scenario building of eating Jelly Belly jelly beans. Anyone who has enjoyed these gourmet beans knows they come in many flavors that usually represent a food, like chocolate pudding, buttered popcorn, peach, bubble gum, orange sherbet, and so on. With most packages of the beans, which feature an assortment of flavors, a little recipe book would come inside. You could find one each of a chocolate, a marshmallow, and a graham cracker Jelly Belly and pop them into your mouth at the same time for a new taste—smores in this case. McGonigal explains that creating scenarios is something like this jelly menu sensation—take some number of the insights you have and combine them to see what comes out. It can be useful to focus on one sector for the creation to focus efforts; it can be hard to formulate ideas without some constraints.[216]

Storyboarding

More than a tweet or a jelly menu sensation, storyboarding includes a narrative and gives a bigger picture. Painting a

---

[216] *SxSW EDU*, "Jane McGonigal | SXSWedu Keynote | How to Think (and Learn) Like a Futurist."

picture through words or images can be a very powerful way to communicate the scenario you think may play out as well as how it may impact the world. In 2019, writer New York Rep. Alexandria Ocasio-Cortez and Naomi Klein released a film on the Intercept's website, "A Message from the Future."[217] You do not have to agree with the representative on issues to understand the effectiveness of the tool in selling a future. What can work well for this method of scenario building is creating a simple storyboard (an empty comic strip, in effect) and drafting out the scenes that tell the story.

Thing from the Future (Situation Lab)

This fun and award-winning card game from the Situation Lab provides some structured scenario-making fun.[218] After you get the hang of how the game is played, you can use blank cards to fill in and create new possibilities.

The object of the game is to come up with the most entertaining and thought-provoking descriptions of hypothetical objects from different near-, medium-, and long-term futures. Each round, players collectively generate a creative prompt by playing a card game. This prompt outlines the kind of future that the thing to be imagined comes from, specifies what part of society or culture it belongs to, describes the type of object that it is, and suggests an emotional reaction it might spark in an observer from the present. Players must

---

217 Naomi Klein, "A Message from the Future with Alexandria Ocasio-Cortez," *The Intercept*, April 17, 2019.
218 Stuart Candy and Jeff Watson, "The Thing from the Future," Situation Lab, accessed February 1, 2020.

then each write a short description of an object that fits the constraints of the prompt.

While the game has long been sold out, you can download and print out a set of cards.[219] There is a video explaining the game by one of the co-creators, Candy, available on Vimeo under his channel (Stuart Candy).[220] If you want to have even more fun while also tapping into more of your creativity, prototype your "things."

Mild to Wild

This can be used from scratch or in combination with the methods above.

Fresh Start: Imagine a scenario of this insight in the future that is not really that exciting, some application of this concept in your day-to-day life. Then, imagine a scenario that seems completely useless or redundant, and one that is simply outrageous. Now, go back to each and try to play down or play up the concept, so you end up with a full spectrum of scenarios, from mild to wild.

Laddering up: Take the scenarios you have created in a previous step and place them along a horizontal line from mild to wild. Where are the gaps? Imagine scenarios that fit those openings.

---

219 Ibid.
220 *Stuart Candy*, "Thing from the Future Card Game," November 11, 2014, video, 20:29.

Pro-level: Create a two-by-two matrix, with the intensity of mild to wild on the horizontal axis and then another value on the y-axis—could be benefit, impact, value, etc. Now place the scenarios you have created from one of the methods above and figure out where they go. Which quadrant does not have many ideas? Imagine scenarios to fill it up.

***

Whatever you do to create possible scenarios from the future, the next chapter will talk about how to make use of what you dreamed up.

And by the way, there is nothing to say you cannot keep creating more scenarios (you probably will!).

9

THINKING ABOUT POTENTIAL

In the last chapter, you took your observations and grouped them, tested them a bit, and used them to dream up some scenarios. Even if that is as far as you get, you armed yourself with grounded thoughts, should you choose to act. Doing a bit more homework will help you make a more informed and even a more persuasive argument. Are you game? Read on.

This chapter is all about looking at scenarios with a 360-degree mirror to find problems and opportunities, and more importantly, to determine the following: What kind of future does it represent?

FULL SPECTRUM THINKING
Looking back at your scenarios, did you capture both the positive *and* the concerning? Chances are, you thought more of one than the other. Reducing unwanted outcomes in favor of better ones requires us to consider both. Let's look at two

examples to show the difference between a single perspective and a two-sided one.

Corporate videos of the future are examples of optimistic (only) futures. Corning's popular five-minute 2011 video "A Day Made of Glass" demonstrated improving ease and increasing enjoyment in day-to-day life through advances in display technology—from the way you wake to the way you work.[221] Watch it and notice how many of these experiences are part of your life today!

An example exploration from SuperFlux at least provides both perspectives. In her 2017 talk, Jain shared a narrative about the experience of living with a drone security guard:[222]

We call it The Nightwatchman. It patrols the streets, often spotted in the evenings and at night. Initially, many of us were annoyed by its low, dull hum. But then, like everything else, we got used to it. Now, what if you could see the world through its eyes? See how it constantly logs every resident of our neighborhood; logging the kids who play football in the no-ballgame area and marking them as statutory nuisances. And then see how it disperses this other group, who are teenagers, with the threat of an autonomously issued injunction. And then there's this giant floating disc called Madison. Its glaring presence is so overpowering, I can't help but stare at it. But it feels like each time I look at it, it knows a little more about me—like it keeps flashing all these adverts at me, as if it knows about

---

221 Corning Incorporated, "A Day Made of Glass...Made possible by Corning. (2011)," February 7, 2011, video, 5:32.
222 Anab Jain, "Why We Need to Imagine Different Futures," filmed April 2017 in Vancouver, B.C., TED video, 14:31.

the holiday I'm planning. I'm not sure if I find this mildly entertaining or just entirely invasive.

This example demonstrates critical thinking along a paradox:

- What do I hope to see—what would be the positive impacts?
- What do I hope not to see—what could go wrong?

No matter your favorite genre of story, I'm sure you are familiar with comedy, drama, and horror. Taking each scenario and channeling your inner screenwriter can be a good way to find those aspects of a future that might not have come to mind before. Simply ask yourself, if this scenario were to show up in a comedy, how would it likely play out—what would be the emerging trope? For drama, you can take one of two paths—miraculous or tragic. With horror, try to channel Badminton, who would say, "don't be afraid to look into the abyss!" The documentary might be the bucket for those scenarios actually already happening today, somewhere in the world, and don't really present much of a change in either a good or bad direction. Scenarios close to what we have today, where the change is just incremental, are referred to as "neutral scenarios."

FRAMING THE SCENARIO

Having conceived a spectrum of developments, framing them requires a bit more thought as to the likelihood of each coming to pass.

Many reading this, especially my fellow project managers, can tell you that the cone of uncertainty is not new. The basic premise of the cone is that we know more about things happening sooner than we do further out. The narrow end is the near term and represents a smaller range of likely/possible events, and the further out, the more it widens, as the set of possibilities expands. Even with the best process and risk management, things change over time, and we are less certain about events of the distant future.

The cone is a familiar construct for futurists. There are many variations on this futures cone, but all seem to be based on the same original source: consulting research done for WHO in the early 1990s. Here, I provide my own interpretation, based on the original and variations of the cone, with key elements added:

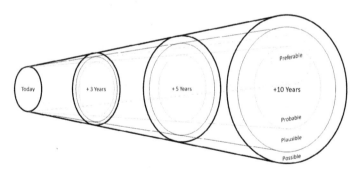

Cones of futures on the horizons.

FEASIBILITY

The three main and concentric rings—possible, plausible, and probable—are characterizations of *feasibility*.

- **Possible** reflects just about anything imaginable, but based on what we know today, isn't likely to happen. These scenarios require some new knowledge to come about in the future for them to materialize—they "transgress the presently accepted 'laws' of science."
- **Plausible** reflects scenarios that may happen because of what we know today and what we think we'll know by tomorrow. Much of what you generated in the last chapter will fall into this category.
- **Probable** are those futures in the line of sight from today because they already exist or are in the process of evolving already. What is forecasted today based on historical data would be included here?

For a scenario to be *more* likely than not—*plausible* rather than simply *possible*—there would be drivers and forces behind change showing up today. When deciding the trajectory for a scenario, think about the kind of factors you considered in making your observations—whether it was PESTLE, TRENDS, or something else—but this time. look at them from a different angle, in the context of what you imagined. For example:

- **Social factors:** What social constructs are required?
- **Economic context:** Are the resources required for this scenario going to be available?
- **Technical feasibility:** Are the components of the scenario understood and on track for development or improvement, if needed?

Let's consider Jain's scenario drone described earlier; she went on to explain how plausible it is:

Whilst drones like Madison and Nightwatchman, in these forms, are not real yet, most elements of a drone future are, in fact, very real today. For instance, facial recognition systems are everywhere— in our phones, even in our thermostats, and in cameras around our cities —keeping a record of everything we do, whether it's an advertisement we glanced at or a protest we attended.

Backcasting is another foresight technique that may take a different name depending on which framework you choose to follow. It might be called unwinding, plan-in-reverse, work-back, etc. The general idea is to figure out what steps are needed to get from A (today) to B (the future scenario) by forecasting *backward* from the future state. So, which activities and milestones would be evident if this is going to happen? My experience shows this typically becomes a back-and-forth dialogue of both what exists today that could evolve and the breaking down of future ideas into components to be created along the way. Going through this exercise may push a future from one circle into another, having tested the plausibility.

THE WILDCARDS

In risk management, the two primary factors of consideration are probability and impact. This basic classification allows a risk manager to decide how to use risk-mitigating resources. There are additional factors, and it is possible to assign values to them for calculating a metricized score of total risk. For the Citizen Futurist, just these two factors are sufficient to learn more.

- High probability, high impact
  - Undesirable future: mitigate as high priority
  - Desirable future: invest and defend as high priority
- High probability, low impact
  - Undesirable future: mitigate or eliminate if resources allow
  - Desirable future: look for opportunities to increase positive impact, as resources allow
- Low probability, high impact
  - Undesirable future: mitigating or eliminating is a moderate priority
  - Desirable future: look for opportunities to increase probability
- Low probability, low impact
  - Undesirable future: mitigating or eliminating is a low priority
  - Desirable future: acting is a low priority

If a scenario is well defined, it is easier to understand the potential impact. What if the probability or impact is not as clear? Indeed, there are different classifications of plausible problems.

In 2002, then-Secretary of Defense Donald Rumsfeld made a series of statements that would go on to be some of the most oft-referenced words in the world of risk management:[223]

As we know, there are known knowns; there are things we know we know. We also know there are known unknowns; we

---

[223] David A. Graham, "Rumsfeld's Knowns and Unknowns: The Intellectual History of a Quip," *The Atlantic*, March 27, 2014.

know there are some things we do not know. But there are also unknown unknowns—the ones we don't know we don't know.

Jared Diamond states eloquently how each of these classifications of risk can lead to major problems:[224]

Human societies and smaller groups make disastrous decisions for a whole sequence of reasons: failure to anticipate a problem, failure to perceive it once it has arisen, failure to attempt to solve it after it has been perceived, and failure to succeed in attempts to solve it.

As you might imagine, the combination of *low* probability and *high* impact is particularly troublesome. This type of wild card is one that strategists have broken down into useful categories:

- A Black Elephant, proposed by Vinay Gupta, is essentially a **known unknown**.[225] For example, there are many who know that infectious diseases pop up all of the time, but no one can really predict when one will emerge that is highly contagious and extremely lethal. As bad as COVID-19 has been, there could be something worse in the future. The elephant in the room.
- The Black Jellyfish, proposed by Sardar and Sweeney, is essentially the **unknown known**.[226] This is, in effect, the

---

224 Diamond, Jared. *Collapse: How Societies Choose to Fail or Succeed.* (New York: Penguin Books, 2011), 277.
225 Mikko Dufva, "The Horizon Scanning Zoo," *Ennakointikupla*, accessed February 24, 2021; Ziauddin Sardar, John A. Sweeney, The Three Tomorrows of Postnormal Times, *Futures* 75, 2016, 1-13.
226 Ibid.

scale of impacts from current events. An example here is the civil rights activities of 2020. While it can be argued that the civil rights movement has been in progress for decades now and that the Black Lives Matter movement started before 2020, the scale and duration of protests in 2020 were not necessarily foreseeable. Social movements dart and move unpredictably, often in response to unforeseen stimuli, like a jellyfish.

- The Black Swan, popularized by Nasim Nicholas Taleb, is the **unknown unknown**.[227] Ironically, it is the identification of a Black Swan that would quickly change its status as such. The Swan represents that which was previously thought fiction or impossible, just like the namesake fowl.

The animal analogies for wildcards have been extended to include more nuanced varieties—from the Cow to the Unicorn, Peacocks to Dodos—but for the purposes of the Citizen Futurist, the three described above are sufficient.

THE INTERSECTIONS

Somewhere in this neatly organized set of futures is the smattering of what will actually happen. On the other side of time, there will be a generous portion of probable, a side of plausible, and perhaps even a sprinkling of possible outcomes. By looking across the entire funnel, finding the best outcomes, and highlighting them as preferable, we can create a focus. Consider the seams between trajectory zones. Where are

---

[227] Nassim Nicholas Taleb, "'The Black Swan: The Impact of the Highly Improbable'," *The New York Times*, April 22, 2007.

the most interesting things going to happen? What might be done to ensure they do?

***

For the many machinations you have made about futures, understanding how to talk about potential will serve to bolster your arguments for or against things to come.

As you consider how to act, keeping potential in mind will also help you prioritize.

10

THINKING PREFERABLE

How can you give as much thought to *which futures are preferable* as you did in every other step so far? Some of your choices may seem obvious to you—but do you know why or what the implications of those choices may be?

AVOIDING A SCARCITY MINDSET

I was recently listening in on a Clubhouse conversation where I heard Emily Schwartz, a water infrastructure advocate, mention it is often a scarcity mindset that holds people back from thinking or acting on the future. This is a fantastic insight and a new lens I suggest you look through when considering which futures to throw your support behind.

What is a scarcity mindset? It is one ruled by the concern for limited resources. The scarcity mindset does have benefits, for "it orients the mind automatically and powerfully toward unfulfilled needs."[228] This means it helps us find those things

---

228 Shahram Heshmat, "The Scarcity Mindset: How Does Being Poor Change the Way We Feel and Think?" *Psychology Today*, April 2, 2015.

that we need to survive as well as those needed to manage priorities, deadlines, and trade-offs. In some contexts, though, when the mind focuses this way, it tends to be guided by fear, and this can lead to any number of bad behaviors. It can result in a vicious circle of decision making; those with few financial resources will spend so much time managing tough decisions that the willpower to spend wisely in times of abundance is just not available—they have strengthened their mental muscle that values the present over the future.

Imagine if those in the *bottom 10 percent* had the benefit of the tools used by the *top 1 percent* in order to ease their cognitive loads when experiencing any level of financial resources.

So, what does the scarcity mindset have to do with futurism and acting on possible futures? My assertion is that we should consider if a scarcity mindset is (or is not) influencing our *selection* of preferable futures. Context directly influences the perceived value of a product, service, or future.

If we focus innovation only around the controlled or equal distribution of limited resources instead of on more efficient distribution, or abundance-creation, we are missing opportunities of high impact.

OPTIMISTIC & DYSTOPIAN IMPLICATIONS
From Candy:

Once you begin to look at the futures as an array of possibilities, as a landscape to be navigated as time goes by—you can begin to ask yourself questions, you can begin to scan the environment looking for signals of change for little seeds of what may come forth—seeds you may decide to water or weeds you may decide to pull out—you can begin to garden change. The most powerful idea in foresight isn't an idea; it's a commitment. The most powerful idea of futures studies is the act of deciding to engage it, of gardening change, of engaging an optimism of the will, and asking what the other possibilities are here?[229]

So, how do you decide which seeds to water and which weeds to pull? You may have an understanding now of just how messy the business of looking into the future can be! It can become more and more overwhelming. In the next chapter, you will begin to shape how you might take action. The purpose of this chapter is to encourage you to advocate primarily for optimistic outcomes, as well as to prompt you to consider influencing society away from the dystopian.

For selecting seeds to water, Sommers suggests beginning with a simple litmus test of desire and risk: "Duh!" (we can easily act on this) or "Love it!" (some time and money to develop), to "OMG!" (a game-changer needing expansion/focus of capabilities).[230] For the weeds, it can be tougher to see, given the varied potential discussed in the last chapter, but it is important to look for both sides of the coin.

The surge pricing for ride shares may seem like fair competition until people frantically trying to get out of a violent

---

[229] Tedx Talks, "Foresight 101. Designing Our Own Futures | Stuart Candy | TEDxBlackRockCity," January 9, 2015, video, 15:19.

[230] Cecily Sommers, *Think Like a Futurist: Know What Changes, What Doesn't and What's Next.*

scene also see outrageous price hikes. Rent-a-bike or rent-a-scooter services have increased mobility in urban centers but also resulted in some cluttered sidewalks or traffic management nightmares. There are dozens of these types of problems—more popping up every day.

In 2018, SuperFlux, creator of the drone futures, set out to create two interactive experiences for an exhibit they called *Stark Choices*. Working with The Varkey Foundation, the simulations provided two different narratives in a world where robots have taken over most jobs. In the dystopian simulation, visitors were informed their position had been declared redundant, and they were herded through narrow corridors, trying to find new jobs in WorkShare, a hypothetical employer for the 99 percent, while staying out of the targets of security drones. In the optimistic simulation, visitors were invited into a welcoming environment and prompted to consider how work can be redefined to free and assist people in healing social divides.[231]

"Where is the line between preferable and dystopian?" I asked Williams. She said it isn't just the dystopian future we need to worry about, but also any utopian scenario that also brings a totalizing (one-size-fits-all, top-down) future. When we give up our agency to companies, we turn over our future to them. The best future is one of a "protopia," she says, where you have more choices and more voices. She credits Kevin Kelly as the source of this concept, in his book *The Inevitable 1*, and commends efforts by major champions like Monica Bielskyte

---

[231] Anab Jain and Jon Ardern, "Stark Choices," Superflux, 2018, accessed February 21, 2021.

for propelling the concept forward.[232] Bielskyte prototypes the future through lenses of optimism and humanitarianism; she says she is working to bridge the gap between scientific research and technological innovation's effect on culture and politics and vice versa.[233]

***

Humans are not wired for change, but we are wired to perceive threats and danger. Imagining dystopian futures can seem like fearmongering, but just as we cannot *create* what we have not imagined, we cannot *avoid* it either. Readers with education in psychology know it is equally important to not *focus* on a negative future, as when we do, we invariably and unintentionally aim right for it. My favorite sitcom example of this is an old episode of *Frasier*, where Frasier was learning to ride a bike. When he focused his eyes on an object he hoped to avoid (be it a tree or mailbox), he would steer right into it, even in the middle of a charity race.[234]

If we consider what negative consequences may come with a possible future, we can start to plan ahead for how to pivot away from it—and this is usually best done by focusing on a preferable future.

---

[232] Kevin Kelly, *The Inevitable: Understanding the 12 Technological Forces That Will Shape Our Future*, (United Kingdom: Penguin Books, 2017).
[233] "Design is [Protopian]," *Google Design*, May 17, 2019, video, 1:00:49.
[234] *Frasier*, "Fraternal Schwinns," season 10, episode 16, February 25, 2003, directed by Sheldon Epps, Paramount, video, 21:00.

PART 4

ACTING ON FUTURES

We choose and create major aspects of the
future by what we do or fail to do.

—ANN TAKET[235]

---

235 Ann Taket, ed., "Health Futures in support of health for all," World Health Organization, July 19-23, 1993.

11

CITIZEN FUTURISTS

The first question to the scientists, during the 2021 annual press briefing on the annual doomsday clock update, came from Michael del Castillo of Forbes: "What action should regular citizens take to ensure the bulletin decision to keep the clock closer to midnight than it has ever been is considered by the governments and businesses that serve them?" Governor Jerry Brown, former governor of California and executive chair of *Bulletin of the Atomic Scientists*, responded first, saying, "the most important thing you can do is that every one of your political representatives knows that nuclear threat is an extreme danger now." Dr. Rachel Bronson, president and CEO of *Bulletin of the Atomic Scientists*, said, "The pandemic has helped us lead the way, where we have been able to see… that individual decisions, when aggregated, can make a powerful difference to keeping political intention on key issues." [236]

---

236 "This Is Your COVID Wake-up Call: It is 100 Seconds to Midnight," *Bulletin of the Atomic Scientists*, January 27, 2011, video, 1:01:51.

So, do not let your good work go to the wayside. Take what you have learned forward and consider these tips for building on what you have started. Many people assume that someone else is taking care of the future for us, but not the Citizen Futurist. It can be overwhelming to consider and respond to every call to action, especially given the always-on internet and its open seas of information. Advocacy and activist efforts are often reduced to changing profile pictures and publishing hash-tagged messages. There is more you can do. By raising your level of intention around the future, you will become a voice for the future and bring others along.

There are different realms of activism: personal, family, community, and global.[237] There are six different levels of activism engagement: observing, following, endorsing, contributing, owning, and leading.[238] Working across all four realms at all levels is not realistic for most people (if not any person), so give some consideration to what your desired outcome is so you can visualize and execute.

Half of Americans have been civically active on social media in some way, as at least one way to start.[239] The British Ecological Society provides these great tips for engaging

---

[237] Marie Goodwin, "The Four Levels: New Story Activism and Burnout," *Resilience*, August 17, 2016.

[238] Gideon Rosenblatt, "The Engagement Pyramid: Six Levels of Connecting People and Social Change," *Groundwire*, February 1, 2010.

[239] Monica Anderson, Skye Toor, Lee Rainie and Aaron Smith, "Public Attitudes Toward Political Engagement on Social Media," Pew Research Center, July 11, 2018,

policymakers; I think they are valid for all types of external stakeholders:[240]

- Get involved
- Understand the policy environment and stay up to date
- Be timely
- Plan your approach
- Tell a relevant and engaging story
- Be a generalist as well as a specialist
- Rid yourself of imposter syndrome
- Be certain about uncertainty
- Be objective
- Remember, science is not everything

Corporations are making decisions about technological products and services that have far-reaching impacts on consumers (with a very homogenous talent base). There is increasing awareness of the need to include the public—a broader and more diverse audience—into the R&D decision-making process. "The interaction between firms and activists is markedly strategic, and episodes of confrontation are often rooted in decisions made by firms."[241] What would it mean to have a technological version of the FDA or the environmental impact statement, where there is thoughtful consideration given before major efforts are pursued? How do we balance caution with the speed of innovation?

---

240 "Top 10 Tips for Engaging and Communicating with Policy Makers," British Ecological Society, accessed February 16, 2021.
241 Alessandro Piazza, "Firm Behavior and Evolution of Activism: Strategic Decisions and the Emergence of Protest in US Communities," *Strategic Management Journal* 41, no. 4 (November 26, 2019).

MAINTAIN AN OPTIMISTIC, FUTURE-ORIENTED MINDSET

KEEP YOUR EYES OPEN

Besides pursuing bigger thinking about their future, a future-minded person pays attention to what needs and opportunities exist around them. Perhaps a parent, child, friend, or neighbor—even an organization you are affiliated with—has a problem or is in need of a service or product that doesn't currently exist, so watching the horizon for solutions to address those needs can help focus what we might be looking for. It was only after my dad passed that I even had the idea of getting my mom an Echo Dot, to give her some sense of company in the house. Soon she was using it for news and weather updates, setting a time, and playing quiz games. Alexa became a small comfort in a difficult time.

PRACTICE

Practice identifying signals. I love to listen to Bloomberg News in the morning because it brings me back to the big picture of what's happening around the world. When something I hear seems part of a bigger pattern, I note it as a possible signal. There are many ways to incorporate this and the other foresight practices into your routine:

- Next time you are planning your family vacation, try the Jelly Belly menu sensation exercise using travelers' interests, and chances are, you will have a cool vacation idea that you wouldn't have come up with before!

- Maybe you are talking with an unhappy employee, and you can help them to think through the various scenarios and possible futures.
- Having a plan doesn't make you fearful or afraid—it makes you smart for conceiving of a future where you need to be prepared. If there's a disaster, do you have water and necessities on hand? If your family members are at school or work, traveling even—how can the group communicate and what contingency plans are needed for dependents, health care, and prescriptions, and so on?
- Incorporate futures curiosity into your hobbies. Recall how Synn started biohacking to incorporate it into her act. My husband began flying drones for fun but doing so led to paid work taking before and after flyover shots of the reconstruction of several holes at a local private golf course.

THINK IN MULTIPLE HORIZONS OF FUTURES

Building the mental muscle of thinking both short- and long-term is one that must at least be done with intention, when not a free-flowing exercise of dreaming and visioning. It is easy to only focus on the next few days or even just a month out. Some can think a year or two ahead, but commonly it is focused on vacations and personal milestones. How often do you think further out? Robbins asserts that people tend to overestimate what they can do in a year but substantially underestimate what they can do in a decade or two.[242]

---

242 John Rampton, "20 Life Changing Quotes by Tony Robbins," *Inc*, July 25, 2016.

Upon reflection, Becker realized how he applies one of McGonigal's techniques in his own life. "Who are you in the future ten years from now?" was the question she asked, Gene explained, and "'*Who could I be?*' is actually a really interesting exercise. Because it's a game, you don't have to take it quite as seriously. I'm creating a character—it's like designing your own avatar. It's a little bit more fun, but it does provoke you to think about, what could I do that would be substantially different as opposed to just following the incremental path that I would otherwise be on."

This is as true for the world as it is our individual lives. "We read the paper every day and pay too much attention to what's happening now, but what's happening over a long arch is also important," says Dimond.[243]

RAISE FUTURES-LITERATE KIDS

Instill and support futures interests of children. Badminton can trace some part of his interest to the book his father had given him in 1980—*The Usborne Book of the Future: A Trip to the Year 2000 and Beyond*, which had any number of exciting prospects—robotics, telecommunications, underwater and lunar colonies, hyper loop, and more. Holman also began his journey at an early age, teaching himself about computers and learning to program, which was a bit challenging in the remoteness of Alaska. He was self-taught because he had to be. He jokes that no one there really understood the promise of computers; as a kid with a computer and a skateboard, he would get admonished equally about spending time with

---

243 Jamie Dimon, "Jamie Dimon—Chairman and CEO of JPMorgan Chase."

either. Still, he acknowledges it was his parents' support of him becoming anything he wanted that led him to where he is today.

Sommers outlined her vision beautifully toward the end of her book:

In my perfect world, everyone would be change literate. Children would be educated in the Four Forces model, and all of their subjects—including history, literature, science—could also be interpreted through the lens of these four force fields. The forces are, in fact, a continuous story that runs through all human endeavors. As the kids grow older, they would be trained in critical thinking and decision making. Teenagers would be rewarded for considering far-reaching consequences of their actions. Young adults would direct their lives by a strong sense of who they are and where they choose to go and return to that anchor of purpose and vision whenever their lives take a turn. And leaders at every level of society—in all sectors—would eschew ideology while holding fast to their values.[244]

Williams shone a light on the danger of painting today as the pinnacle and that the future will somehow be less than it is today. Whether we are talking climate, equality, political systems, or even education and jobs, suggesting there will not be change for the better "steals" their future because you are taking away agency by doing so, she explains. The chance

---

244 Cecily Sommers, *Think Like a Futurist: Know What Changes, What Doesn't and What's Next*, 215.

that there could be a better future is what will motivate our children to claim agency and pursue impactful lives.

Now, I acknowledge that parents and teachers already have a million things they are trying to remember to teach, instill, and inspire. As a parent of two children born seven years apart, I appreciate that it can be challenging. I encourage you to make futures literacy one of your priorities. That goes for your nieces and nephews, for that matter; my nephew tells me he appreciates our many conversations about the future and finding creative ways to move forward. In those moments of despair or discomfort in ambiguity, shining the light toward what is ahead and what is possible can be very powerful. When young adults begin looking at alternatives to college programs, use the opportunity to talk longer term and offer insights you have gained about what might be coming, or where new gaps in skills and careers are likely to be. I believe that Rinne's message—learn to have a healthy relationship with change—is perhaps the most important skill you can gift to your children through role modeling and teaching.

I will be the first to say I have not excelled at this as a parent up until now. My goal has been to constantly express there are many different possible futures, that it is never too late to try something new, to pivot, to try to make an impact or influence what may happen. I continue to teach both of them as young adults as I learn more.

MOVE UP THE ADOPTION CURVE

We have all developed behaviors based on our level of comfort with new products and innovation. My dad warned me never to buy the first year of a new car model, for instance. Many of you might have that friend who is buying every new product that comes out and takes pride in being the first to have it. Those first-to-have-it friends of yours may be innovators in the industry, or they may be technophile early adopters. Most consumers get on board after something has become more established, and many wait until it's widely available. Taking part in discussions of the future requires understanding what is available today.

PRIORITIZE THE FUTURE

To better serve our future selves and stop treating ourselves so poorly, we have to make the future a priority. Sommers gives organizations the guidance of investing 5 percent of resources in the future. If large corporations can be successful betting just 5 percent, do you think you could too? Imagine you dedicate 5 percent of your waking time each week to the future. For the average eight-hour-a-night sleeper, that means that you dedicate (and fiercely protect) about five and a half hours per week focused on the future. Less than an hour a day to make sure you are better off in the future![245]

Holman emphasized that solutions will come, and younger generations will pursue them; your vote is in how quickly you want it solved and if you want to contribute.

---

245 Cecily Sommers, *Think Like a Futurist: Know what Changes, What Doesn't and What's Next*, 198.

VOTE FOR FUTURE-MINDED LEADERS

Today, government leaders are falling behind science and technology in creating policies. Anyone who watched US congressional hearings with tech companies in recent years likely saw that many of our leaders are completely out of touch with social media, software, and technology. "How do you sustain a business model in which users don't pay for your service?" asked Senator Hatch—self-acknowledged 2010 chair of the Senate Republican High-Tech Task Force—of Mark Zuckerberg (who responded that they run ads).[246] Representative Ted Poe pushed Google CEO Sundar Pichai to answer a simple yes or no to if Poe's iPhone lets Google track his movement (this answer is not binary; it depends if Google is even installed and what settings are enabled).[247] "The moment was emblematic of a hearing in which representatives' zeal for grandstanding was often undermined by their technological illiteracy," writes Will Oremus.[248]

You may not understand why these questions are absurd, but you are probably not holding hearings and trying to determine what, if any, legislation or government investments should include. Representative Kinzinger (and others) admitted in a hearing on the promise of quantum computing that he only understood about 50 percent of what was being presented.[249] In the same hearing, Representative Bucshon spoke to the challenge of communicating the importance of

---

246 Mark Zuckerberg, "Transcript of Mark Zuckerberg's Senate hearing," transcribed by Bloomberg, April 10, 2018.
247 Will Oremus, "Google's Web of Confusion," *Slate*, December 11, 2018.
248 Ibid.
249 "Quantum Computing," House Energy Subcommittees on Environment and Digital Commerca & Consumer Protection hearing, streamed by CSPAN, May 18, 2018, video, 1:22:00.

an innovation, even when understood, to constituents—he asks for the basic elevator pitch. Kennedy also asked for input on how to respond to skeptics of the field.[250]

O'Shea and I spoke about the technical gap. "A lot of our politicians don't understand emerging technology and science—we need a more informed populace and in turn a more informed electorate," he says. "To solve the problems we are facing, it's going to take more techno-literacy."

To be fair, representatives must be generalists and rely on a support staff for specializations. Congress used to have a technical think tank called the Office of Technology Assessment from the 1970s until 1995, but the House shut it down in a large government reduction imitative.[251] There have been efforts made ever since to restore the group; proponents have cited the value of having the group, which provided balanced reports on hundreds of topics. Celia Wexler of the *New York Times* wrote in 2015 about the need to revive the office. She noted that the office gained international acclaim with the quality of its work and that this work included a report that led to mammograms and pap smears being covered by Medicare, the reliability of polygraph testing, more accurate cost assessments of synthetic fuels in the 1970s, and the "Star Wars" missile defense system in the 1980s.[252] Moreover, the group paid for itself in hundreds of millions of dollars in

---

250 Ibid.
251 Celia Wexler, "Bring Back the Office of Technology Assessment," *The New York Times*, May 28, 2015.
252 Ibid, Tim Beardsley, "Strategic Defense Initiative: Star Wars Criticized by OTA Report," *Nature* 317, no. 6035, September 1985.

savings even through something as simple as the government's computer procurement plan.²⁵³

Some members of Congress and presidential candidates announced moves to try to restore the office in recent years. Others have resisted, mostly those having a long history of questioning science and suspicion of tech. Rush Holt, with a PhD in physics from New York, former arms control expert for the State Department, and five-time *Jeopardy* winner, who also once beat IBM's Watson supercomputer, arrived on Capitol Hill in 1999 and was alarmed by the lack of science and technology literacy.²⁵⁴ He tried to bring back OTA in 2001, 2006, and 2009. In 2009, he penned a press release that included praise for the forward-looking work of the office. "By 1995, for example, OTA already had written on such topics, now current, as 'Electronic Surveillance in a Digital Age' and the 'Potential Environmental Impacts of Bioenergy Crop Production.'"²⁵⁵ Holt retired from Congress in 2015, and he now heads the American Association for the Advancement of Science, an organization that places expertise in congressional offices funded by science organization sponsorships. Requests for these fellows outpaces two-fold the number available. Another organization, TechCongress, places professionals in personal and committee staffs. Is this patchwork solution best?²⁵⁶

---

253 Celia Wexler, "Bring Back the Office of Technology Assessment."
254 Grace Gedye, "How Congress Got Dumb on Tech—and How It Can Get Smart," *Washington Monthly*, April-June 2019.
255 Rush Holt, "Statement of the Representative Holt on the Office of Technology Assessment," The House of Representatives (press release), February 14, 2009.
256 Grace Gedye, "How Congress Got Dumb on Tech—and How It Can Get Smart."

While it tends to be Republicans who balk at the value and intentions of scientists and technologists, there has been bipartisan support to restore this office. The fact is that without it, legislators are left to rely on sometimes biased outside organizations or holding hearings of industry leaders who will also have a slanted point of view. And while I have highlighted the problems with support and resources for legislators, the issue isn't the OTA alone; *Washington Monthly* adds that the 1995 changes "took an ax to the entire congressional nervous system." Other key research and support services were cut 25–45 percent. This means that the remaining staff of generally inexperienced political scientists making on average fifteen dollars an hour have huge portfolios of issues and topics to manage.[257]

Amy Webb is pushing for a National Office of Strategic Foresight. Her opening statement reads, "Despite an abundance of technical experts across its agencies, the federal government lacks a centralized office charged with long-range, comprehensive, streamlined planning to address critical science and technology developments."[258]

To affect change, you must vote. In 2016, voter turnout was 55.4 percent, the lowest in twenty years.[259] In 2020, it is estimated 66 percent of eligible voters turned out, the highest

---

257 Ibid.
258 Amy Webb, "A National Office for Strategic Foresight Anchored in Critical Science and Technologies," Stanford Geopolitics, Technology and Governance Cyber Policy Center, October 17, 2019.
259 Gregor Wallace, "Voter Turnout at 20-year Low in 2016," *CNN*, November 30, 2016.

since 1900—but is this enough?[260] These proportions are from presidential elections, which get the most voter attention, but midterm and local voting, it can be argued, is far more important and have markedly lower turnout. While our turbulent politics have been challenging, it has resulted in an increase in the level of civic engagement—I hope this can be a lasting effect.

Voting is a right, but it carries with it a responsibility to become more educated on issues and candidates. Jain talks about how Brexit voters soon were "Bregeters"—they voted for it without thinking through the consequences.[261] Educate yourself and elect future-oriented leaders. Futures-literate leaders will consider what is possible for our community and steer us toward better outcomes than those who are passionate about keeping the status quo.

LOOK, THINK, AND ACT TOGETHER

Consider bringing futures chat to your book club, or if you are not part of one, consider starting one. The book club is a great place to discuss futures and might also be the perfect set of people to try out some of the activities described in this book.

This is true not just for book clubs, but for PTAs, local Meetup groups, professional organizations, and more; selecting a topic and finding a presenter or materials to review can be a great way to bring these discussions to the broader

---

260 Andrea Park, "2020 Voter Turnout Was the Highest the US Has Seen in Over a Century," *Marie Claire*, November 5, 2020.
261 Anab Jain, "Why We Need to Imagine Different Futures."

public. Speaking of acting with your PTA, use the leverage of your association to ask schools to provide sufficient arts and humanities content, so our future scientists and engineers have that well-rounded education that includes ethics and foresight.

If hosting and entertaining is something you love to do, think about bringing futures discussions to your routine. You might recall from earlier in the book the throwback to a dining society called Ratio Club, where scientists like Alan Turing and Grey Walter were known to share their thinking. Consider hosting a dinner party with the goal of conducting futures-focused conversations.

ENGAGING STAKEHOLDERS

Some citizens have become more consciences about consumption and have been effective in applying pressure to companies to be more environmentally friendly. People have marched for days, weeks, and months to sound off for civil rights, which has made a difference, from incremental to monumental changes. It is possible to make a difference even with behemoth organizations.

My first advice is to be well prepared—make it easier to deliver more signal than noise to stakeholders. If you feel compelled to engage with an organization stakeholder directly, make sure you have done your homework. Dimon, in the Fisher podcast, said he welcomes input from anyone but asks for that input to be informed. "People's attention span has gotten shorter. People read less. People will rant about something and say you guys should do A, B, and C. So, when I say we do A, B and C, they say, well, I didn't know about that. Well, you didn't know about it because you didn't read. You didn't take the time."[262]

Support Futures-Focused Non-Profits

Support can come in many forms, not just financial. Attend and promote events, connect like-minded people and groups, participate in dialogues on social media—these are all ways you can help further the mission of a group that you support.

You can also help by making your voice heard online independently. Write, film, and be heard online, through social media, blogs, and videos—and support others who do as well.

***

You have demonstrated interest and commitment by reading this far. I have no doubt you will succeed in pursuing whatever futures you can imagine (as preferable, of course).

Be confident, optimistic, and vocal about possible futures.

---

262 Jamie Dimon, "Jamie Dimon—Chairman and CEO of JPMorgan Chase."

12

STUDENTS AND EDUCATORS

Candy explains, "We don't need batteries of experts—not a culture of expertise but a social capacity, a civilizational ability to think well about futures and choose more wisely from among them. We need to distribute this capacity among us."[263]

Education is not immune to innovation and changes, so while I focus on the traditional academic setting here, I also note that there are many different onramps to careers today. Education is in the middle of a dramatic transformation. Skills are outdated too fast for it not to. When I graduated high school, before the internet took over, there was not the same access to seeing and understanding the wide variety of paths one could take. Education is a two-way contract—Universities need to be nimble and current in their

---

263 *TEDx Talks*, "Foresight 101. Designing our own futures | Stuart Candy | TEDxBlackRockCity."

pedagogy, and students need to own their academic careers. So here are two discussions on education aimed at each end of that agreement.

STUDENTS

It can be overwhelming to consider the many options available to you today. My advice to mentees, students, my children, and nephews has been to start *somewhere* and to be ready to pivot. I realize that many people have been wildly successful by plotting a course and sticking with it, but pivoting has generally worked out for just as many. You can utilize the tools and resources in this book to help you imagine your own futures and to figure out education that fits in.

K–12

For science and technology specifically, there are now a plethora of STEM programs available. While some like Webb argue that this is a generational gaffe, that younger digitally-native generations do not need to be made aware of tech; someone like Adesanya would suggest that the programs are still critical—as they create interest in building tech, not just using tech. Make sure you are looking for programs that explore the "why" as much as they teach the "how." There are other opportunities that will help build skills of future literacy and a dialogue of discourse. If your school or community offers any courses, after-school programs, or other types of extracurricular activities that encourage questioning, researching, imagining, and expressing—these are valuable resources for you. Be they music and arts, marketing, social sciences, history and debates, or even philosophy. All of these forward-thinking and humanities-based educational opportunities will make you a stronger, well-rounded, and resilient Citizen Futurist. Many today are realizing that there is a core set of skills for futures thinking that are needed to thrive in society—personal finance with topics like insurance, budgeting, and planning, civic engagement from how to obtain a license to registering and voting, and more. For whatever reason, not everyone graduates high school or leaves home with these basic life skills. That needs to change.

POST-SECONDARY

If you are looking to be in design or business strategy, look for programs that incorporate foresight and/or futures studies into the program—or, if you are already enrolled in one that does not push your school to create an offering. Because I worked in creative teams for several years, I came to know of foresight as a specialization. Had I really known sooner about this, I would have likely really homed in on research and foresight much earlier. If you have already decided that futures is what you want to pursue more formally, there are two domestic programs for those in the US, and futures studies programs can be found around the world.

The Hawaii Research Center for Futures Studies (*Hawaii Futures*) was established by the Hawaii State Legislature in 1971. According to the Center:

Located within the Department of Political Science, College of Social Sciences at the University of Hawaii at Manoa, it has been instrumental in the education of four decades of futurists, in the development and spread of judicial and educational foresight, and in bringing foresight and futures thinking to organizations, agencies, and businesses around the world. Each of us has an essential role in the construction of whatever futures do come to pass. Humans have never before had more influence over—and ethical responsibilities toward—the futures of our environment, our biology, and indeed, of all life. Futures studies encourages the contemplation of many possible futures and facilitates dialogue between groups with competing or conflicting visions.[264]

And at the University of Houston, there is a graduate program in Studies of the Future. It was established in 1974 by Dean of Human Sciences and Humanities, Calvin Cannon, and Chancellor of UH-Clear Lake, Alfred Neumann. The program shares this overview:

Professional futurists emphasize systemic and transformational change as opposed to traditional forecasters and planners who focus on incremental change based on existing conditions and trends. Since long-term predictive forecasts are rarely correct, futurists describe alternative plausible and preferable futures, in addition to the expected future. Instead of limiting themselves to traditional forecasters' quantitative methods, futurists also use a balance of qualitative and quantitative tools. The program provides collaboration and innovation with multiple perspectives on foresight, business and marketing, and consumer science and retailing.[265]

---

264 "Alternative Futures," Department of Political Science, College of Social Sciences, University of Hawai'i, Mānoa.
265 "Program," College of Technology, Foresight Program, University of Houston, accessed February 21, 2021.

I was delighted to learn that Arizona State University, where I started my five-school-one-bachelor-degree journey, now has a Consortium for Science, Policy, and Outcomes.[266]

The Consortium for Science, Policy, and Outcomes is an intellectual network aimed at enhancing the contribution of science and technology to society's pursuit of equality, justice, freedom, and overall quality of life. CSPO creates knowledge and methods, cultivates public discourse, and fosters policies to help decision-makers and institutions grapple with the immense power of science and technology as society charts a course for the future.

Some schools offer independent study; you might be able to use this option to focus on foresight. If your institution has an Interdisciplinary Arts and Sciences program, you can explore the many different types of programs that provide the best blend for Futures. If you have your mind made up to be in a technical program, push to make room for electives in humanities, including cultural studies and ethics. Badminton was able to find and attend a really cool hybrid program for applied psychology and computing. It included cognitive psychology, organizational psychology, social psychology, human-computer interaction, artificial intelligence, and linguistics.

Even if your school doesn't have many options, hope is not lost. Schools like Arizona State University also have cross-campus research and engagement opportunities, such

---

266 "Consortium for Science, Policy and Outcomes," Arizona State University, accessed February 21, 2021.

as a Center for Technology, Data, and Society, as well as a Center for Science, Technology, and Environment Policy Studies.[267]

EDUCATORS

FORESIGHT CULTURE

While there perhaps should be more college programs for foresight and future studies, full programs are not necessarily needed everywhere; there is any number of ways that futures literacy could be incorporated into curriculums, student life, and special events. Besides educating the future professionals of the world, universities are responsible for tremendous achievements in research, and this includes possible futures. Interdisciplinary conferences are sometimes held for discussion and consensus on what the future may look like. Candy works with students at Carnegie Mellon University to design artifacts and experiences "from" the future to feel the way into what these possibilities may portend and let it inform our decisions to date. [268]

Pulling people into foresight and innovation isn't always through an academic program, but rather the adjacent activities—so provide opportunities for students to stumble on things. It is imperative to give students that space for discovery. Becker shared some of the memorable experiences that provided the spark for him:

---

267 "Research Centers," Arizona State University, accessed March 15, 2021.
268 "Stuart Candy," Carnegie Mellon University, accessed March 15, 2021.

I was lucky enough to get into MIT. Interestingly enough, the innovation education I got was really more from prowling the halls of MIT at night and on weekends, rather than necessarily the formal coursework. It was stumbling on the exhibit of Doc Edgerton's strobe photography where he's taking those famous shots of bullets going through apples or stumbling onto some of the first interactive computer terminals. Sitting in somebody's lab doing a little odd job, wire-wrapping boards for a few bucks, and seeing that the grad students were all playing some online game that was Space War or something. And I was sitting up until two in the morning playing text-based Adventure on one of the time-sharing systems. Those were the sorts of things that were like, oh, wow, that's a really interesting idea; where did that come from? How did that get built? And I guess I've always felt that fascination, but it kind of got sparked there.

You might expect nothing less from an institution like MIT, but there is plenty of evidence of creating this environment in a multitude of places, even beyond the edges of campus. Access to opportunities for experimentation and the mashing of ideas is not only a logistical concern—students have to have time and mental bandwidth to pursue it. If students are so busy with full loads and programmed social time, they won't have that.

For schools looking to add foresight courses or complete programs, they can look to the University of Houston and University of Hawaii programs, mentioned before as models. There are incredible programs internationally as well, and the

World Futures Studies Federation has accreditation services and pedagogy design resources.[269]

On YouTube, you can find an academically run futurist exercise held at the University of Pittsburgh in 1967, the documentary hosted by the beloved journalist Walter Cronkite. Participants in the futures exercise include names you probably recognize: Isaac Asimov, science fiction writer and professor of bio-chem at Boston University, and Gerard Piel, the well-known publisher and chairman of *Scientific American*.[270]

To create the futuristic landscape, two ten-sided dice were rolled to simulate the probability of a given factor being present. The factors that scored a high probability in the roll were combined to create the imaginary landscape of the year 2000. The new story didn't explain the process used to generate the list of factors, but here is a partial list of the factors they considered.

Do you recognize any of these as concepts present in the past two decades?

- Cooperative international ocean farming
- Decline in supernatural beliefs
- Teaching by direct recording on brain
- Control of people through symbiosis
- Growing bureaucracies
- Canned lectures by eminent professors on TV

---

269 "WFSF in Brief," World Futures Studies Federation, accessed February 1, 2021.
270 reelblack, "The Futurists (1967) | Scientists Predict the 21st Century," December 15, 2018, video, 25:11.

- Tactical behavior control devices
- Improved economies of developing nations
- Territorial claims over ocean portions
- Creation of new types of employment
- Weather control as a military weapon
- Application to agriculture and protein manufacture
- Legislative control of genetic operations
- Increased replacement of human services
- Use of orbital stations for economic purposes
- Personality controlled drugs
- Household robots
- Fertility control
- Hundred-year lifespan
- Controlled thermonuclear power
- Continued automation
- Genetic control
- Household robots
- Wideband communications
- Opinion control
- Further globalization

The participants all have interesting backgrounds they can bring to bear; one member in particular—Bertrand De Jouvenel, a French economist—was the director of a group called the Futuribles. Futuribles was established in 1960, and though De Jouvenel passed in 1987, the group still exists as what may be the longest-running consultancy today:

It is our conviction that, to act freely and construct the future of our organizations and societies, attention to—and understanding of—current developments is primordial. Our work, therefore, consists of detecting, analyzing, and understanding the major forms of current change, identifying the principal uncertainties, devising processes of decision-making and action that incorporate a long-term view and high-level actor involvement in the construction of the future.[271]

MAKE ROOM FOR HUMANITIES
Yes, on the heels of proposing that students need space, I am also going to point out what is missing from programs. There is a serious need to find a way for programs to provide a well-rounded education for innovators. Science, technology, engineering, and math are critical for the *how*, but they don't give you the *why*; or more importantly—the *should we*? Webb has talked about how difficult it is to get humanities subjects into already-packed technical programs: "There's no room," she says, "for cultural studies, ethics," which is why her institute makes tools freely available.[272]

Design and business strategy programs typically incorporate foresight to some extent, but there is a challenge in only having certain types of professionals bring the voice of the future to what become strained conversations (and working relationships). Everyone needs to possess basic foresight skills for the right dialogue and discourse in making decisions about the very inventions that will shape who we are as humans, as a society, and as living creatures on Earth. At a minimum, any school that runs an interdisciplinary arts and sciences program or school and doesn't already advocate for futures-friendly program designs should.

---
271 "Who Are We?" *Futuribles*, accessed March 15, 2021.
272 Amy Webb, "The Big Nine: The Future of AI," filmed at Columbia Business School, August 15, 2019, video, 23:01.

Universities can help conduct the research needed to establish values and protocols for certain segments of innovation. For example, in January 2016, MIT rolled out its "moral machine" online. The moral machine was a platform for gathering a human perspective on moral decisions made by machine intelligence, such as self-driving cars. MIT generated moral dilemmas, where a driverless car must choose the lesser of two evils, such as killing two passengers or five pedestrians. As an outside observer, people would judge which outcome they think is more acceptable. They can then see how their responses (and value assessments) compare with other people. The study was concluded in July 2020.[273]

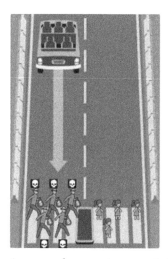 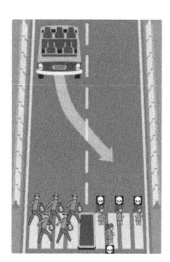

An example scenario presented with the online MIT moral machine experiment.[274]

---

273 Edmond Awad, Sohan Dsouza, Azim Shariff, Jean-François Bonnefon, Iyad Rahwan, "Project Moral Machine," MIT Media Lab, accessed February 20, 2021.
274 Image © The Moral Machine Team: Edmond Awad, Sohan Dsouza, Azim Shariff, Jean-François Bonnefon, Iyad Rahwan. Used with permission.

***

Post-secondary institutions have always been a place where students and educators alike can shine a light on the road ahead, and this has never been more important than it is today. Some futurists like Williams regularly volunteer to help bring foresight into the classroom and learning environments. You can find her many contributions around the web.

Pursue, inspire, and teach futures literacy.

13

ORGANIZATION LEADERS

As a reader of this book, I suspect you already prioritize strategy, planning, and foresight in your teams and organizations (or plan to). What I hope to make clear are the considerations for how to embrace the concepts of bridge making, futures literacy, and citizen futurism.

The performance expectations for companies have changed dramatically over the past twenty years: constant growth fed by continuous innovation, increased diversity in staff and leadership, purposeful products and services, and circular supply chains—the list keeps growing. In the age of COVID, a firm's ability to flex and pivot took center stage. According to *Forbes* writer Georgette Zinaty, the traditional bottom line (that eventually doubled and tripled as industries added people and planet, turned quadruple bottom line with the addition of purpose) now has to account for *pivot*, creating the quintuple bottom line—the now five "P's" are profit, people, planet, purpose, and *pivot*.[275]

Fortunately, those firms that adopt such strategies do see a pay-off:

- Innovative companies outperform others—Mezrich's "Innovation Index," which tracks companies who invest heavily in research and development, outperform the S&P 500 and NASDAQ or even major tech brands by 5–10 percent.[276]
- Diverse organizations increase innovation revenue by 45 percent, highly ethnically diverse organizations outperform at a rate of 35% percent, and gender-diverse organizations outperform by 15 percent.[277]
- According to the *Harvard Business Review*, "Eighty-nine percent of executives surveyed said a strong sense of collective purpose drives employee satisfaction; 84 percent said it can affect an organization's ability to transform, and 80 percent said it helps increase customer loyalty." [278]

---

275 Georgette Zinaty, "High Five: Making the Pivot Part of Your Quintuple Bottom Line," *Forbes*, December 28, 2020.
276 Paul R. La Monica, "Innovative Companies are Trouncing the Rest of the Market," *CNN Business*, May 20, 2019.
277 Ruchika Tulshyan, "Racially Diverse Companies Outperform Industry Norms by 35%," *Forbes*, January 20, 2015; Vijay Eswaran, "The business case for diversity in the workplace is now overwhelming," *World Economic Forum*, April 29, 2019.
278 "The Business Case for Purpose," Harvard Business Review Analytic Services, 2015.

- According to a variety of sources, a majority of sustainability-focused firms see a net-positive increase in financial performance.[279]
- *Entrepreneur Magazine* wrote how companies like Best Buy and Walgreens were able to pass the "pivot-or-die test" during the pandemic; and the *LA Times* found stories of agility in small businesses to avoid closure.[280]

BUILD A CULTURE OF BRIDGE MAKING

In my experience, silos exist in nearly every organization, and this tends to be the source of a myriad of problems that have been compounded by the challenges of a distributed and remote workforce. This compartmentalization issue goes beyond the walls of the firm or industry, too. Bridge-making is needed for all of those gaps to form effective connections and pathways.

Centralized or de-centralized? Flat or pyramid? Matrix? Over the years, I have been in many different types of organizational structures. All have their pros and cons, yet all require clarity, transparency, and great communication to succeed. No matter what strategy your organization or team has taken, bridge-making will make it more healthy and higher performance. Look for places that currently have only one-way communication and consider if a feedback loop would add value. Where teams and levels are differentiated by authority and access, which work against equity and

---

[279] "The Bottom Line on Sustainability," Project Management Institute, 2011, accessed February 20, 2021.

[280] Priya Merchant, "Pivoting During the Pandemic: How These Businesses Succeeded," *Entrepreneur*, January 12, 2021.

belonging, perform an analysis to see if those differences are truly needed. Explicitly expect and reward empowering and enabling collaborative partnerships across invisible lines and analyze situations that have been negatively characterized as analysis paralysis or decision by committee.

Companies that develop strong relationships with academia make the world better. Aumiller shared that a colleague had recently attended MIT's multi-disciplinary conference on ethics and technology. Companies often have travel and training policies that prevent this type of engagement, and this is leaving behind a great opportunity to bring outside thinking into the innovation decision-making process. I have seen where these types of relations are instead preserved for senior leaders, so then the challenge is ensuring that information is distilled well to the people making the product.

EQUITY AND BELONGING

There is still a long way to go for bridge-making between people, beyond the ideological differences touched on earlier. The phrase "diversity and inclusion" has unfortunately been widely misused, including inauthentic and ineffective efforts made to check public relations and recruiting boxes rather than only those efforts that lead to intentional, meaningful change.[281] This can be said of other corporate initiatives, of course, and a bad program can be more harmful to employer trust than having no program at all. According to *Human Resource Executive* Lauren Romansky, managing vice

---

281 Michael J. O'Brien, "Most D&I Programs are Ineffective. Here's How to Change That," *Human Resource Executive*, November 5, 2019.

president in the Gartner HR practice, says that "we know that many D&I strategies are ineffective because they rely on a point-in-time training, an individual champion, or a singular experiment."[282]

Diversity is a demographic descriptor and misses on the characterization of equality between the various representations. While Merriam-Webster includes the "state of being included" in the definition of *inclusion*, it is used as a term for the directional act by some of privilege more than the sense of belonging by every individual.[283] The widely circulated quote from Verna Myers, "Diversity is being invited to the party, inclusion is being asked to dance."[284]

This is a great quote and has served in a powerful way; in a real-life scenario, there is a great deal of complexity in the context that will determine if it results in a sense of belonging. The Equity Institute, here in my home state of Washington, developed a useful tool called the "equity audit window" for schools that may be of use to any organization. It includes a comprehensive look across the institution, instruction, policy, practice, and more.[285]

Adesanya made it into the prestigious engineering program at Purdue University yet did not receive any offers for internships while in attendance, despite going to the engineering

---

282 Ibid.
283 *Merriam-Webster Dictionary Online*, s.v. "inclusion," accessed March 16, 2021.
284 "Diversity Doesn't Stick Without Inclusion," The Vernā Meyers Company, February 4, 2017.
285 "Equity Audit Window," Equity Institute, accessed February 20, 2021.

roundtables every year and bringing a lot of passion; generally, he was told there was no "culture fit." This phrase is enemy one for diversity and inclusion. When you recruit for your organization, partnerships, internal and external teams—diversity means finding different voices and backgrounds for "culture add." Adesanya, being a bridge maker, did not let that stop him from progressing; he took the opportunity to pursue research with Purdue faculty on a mesh node sensor system that would transmit key data from crops through node-to-node transmission. He took his work to the NSBE (National Society of Black Engineers) national undergraduate student technical research competition—and won!

Any efforts to imagine, visualize, and influence outcomes for preferable futures must include a comprehensive scan for movement toward equity and belonging—internally and externally, impacts to a diverse spectrum of communities and people and account for broad definitions in the selection of preferable futures.

BUILD A CULTURE OF FUTURES LITERACY
What does a futures literate organization culture look like? Organizations that develop a healthier relationship with change, failure, and team agency will certainly fare better in the long run.

POWER OF THE PIVOT
An organizational competency of pivoting is founded in a healthy relationship with change. I talked extensively about change in Part 1 of this book at a personal level. With regards

to change in the organization, how you talk about and frame change really matters. One of my favorite TEDx talks on change is by Jason Clarke, titled "Embracing Change." In his video, Clarke talks about seven classic reactions of resistance that humans have to unexpected change and how to mitigate them, including:

- *I'm too full of emotion and fear to think.* For this audience, steering a conversation toward defining the positive, negative, and interesting outcomes, then focusing energy on what is interesting, can be very effective and create a more positive perception of what is coming.
- *I'm scared of the transition, not the idea.* To respond to this, talking honestly about the journey, how turbulent it is going to be, and setting expectations.
- *I don't know how big a deal this change really is.* To mitigate this, talk honestly about the destination—figure out the "four doors," Clarke explains:
  - Business as usual
    - Things we used to be able to do and still can (open door)
    - Things we couldn't do before but still can (closed door)
  - Let it go: things we used to be able to do but can't now (closed door)
  - Go for it: things we couldn't do before but can now (open door)
- *I don't see how I fit into any of this.* Here is the difference between authorship and ownership, Clarke asserts—the former is empowering, and the latter is not. Just as you would talk to consumers of your products and services, include your staff in the conversation. Let them help

decide, given a stated desired outcome, what needs to stay the same, what needs to stop, what should change, and what needs to start happening—give them authorship.
- *I'm fed up with phony change*; I want the real thing. Here Clarke paints a pay-off table for those who are open or closed-minded about change, where a closed mind gives up the opportunity of real change just for the right to say, "I told you so."[286]

The ability for an organization to create an environment where every change is positively framed is a game-changer. When you think about the need to remain nimble, processes and infrastructure change significantly. The change from the Waterfall mindset to the Agile mindset has created a foundation, and the move from physical to digital systems has made rapid change possible. But none of this matters if the culture is not helping people embrace change.

GROWTH MINDSET

Part of why people are resistant to change is the deeply engrained preference for what is known and happening now, often found in a fixed mindset. The antithesis of a fixed mindset is what Carol Dweck calls a growth mindset.[287] What is a better example of the power of the growth mindset to transform than Microsoft? If the mind-blowing market results by the company in the last eight years are not enough proof for you, talk to employees who have been at the

---

286 *TEDx Talks*, "TEDxPerth—Jason Clarke—Embracing Change," December 22, 2010, video, 18:03.
287 Stanford Alumni, "Developing a Growth Mindset with Carol Dweck," October 9, 2014, video, 9:37.

company for more than eight years to hear about the transformation under Satya Nadella's leadership. I have spoken to many who were inspired to stay or return because of the new environment of collaboration and lack of the fear that used to be an underlying current.

According to Dweck, the growth mindset is "not yet" rather than "now."[288] Sounds like a bridge to me! Recognizing and rewarding the strategy, focus, persistence, and learning helps people think about what is possible, rather than what is not. What *is not* is seen as failure, such as a lack of intelligence, talent, ability, or potential. The *not yet* mindset is one of abundance, the *is not* mindset is a scarcity mindset, of fear of not having. Create a culture that empowers the "not yet" and builds a bridge to what is possible.

FORESIGHT IS THE RESPONSIBILITY OF ALL
An organization's ability to identify futures around a product or service requires a diverse set of minds to consider and advise. Strategists and risk managers are likely the most skilled in foresight, but they should not be the only ones who look for possible futures. Williams rejects the notion that only some people have the power to envision futures; "It is an innate human capability," she says. While those disciplines have more technical knowledge around strategies and more experience with speaking in foresight, futures literacy should be developed and recognized throughout the organization and not guarded as something only certain people get to do.

---

288 Ibid.

The benefit of having skilled talent in-house is the opportunity to apply it more widely and to teach others the set of skills. Thinking about the future isn't just about product and service offerings, it's also about the employee, partner, board of directors, etc. Their experiences matter. Changes to the way of working and related workplace trends were accelerated during COVID, including the shift to more flexible and remote work. "Seventy-four percent of companies plan to shift permanently to more remote work," reports Leonhard.[289]

For foresight, you can turn to many agencies, like Fjord of Accenture Interactive, Webb's the Future Today Institute, the Institute for the Future where McGonigal works her magic, International Futures Forum, and SuperFlux in the UK, or Flux Trends in South Africa. Freelance professionals in foresight, like many of the independent futurists featured in this book, such as Nikolas Badminton, April Rinne, or Cecily Sommers, work with organizations to do foresight work, teach foresight skills, or both.

For the organization, foresight will be strengthened with ethnographical research. In a positive trend, many organizations have come to appreciate the value of including full-time anthropologists on their staff. Segmentation has changed. We no longer look at demographics; instead, we look at behaviors, cultures, disciplines, mental models, and relationships. But again, it's the *discussion and engagement* about these factors that is important—not just the *research*.

---

289 *Gerd Leonhard*, "Ten Essential Future Foresights for a Post Corona World: A Covid-19 Virtual Keynote by Gerd Leonhard," June 22, 2020, video, 47:48.

If building up skills in-house is what you aim to do, you can recruit graduates of the University of Houston's Foresight Program or University of Hawaii's Futures Studies—these are, as of this writing, the only two official programs in the US; internationally, you will find more excellent programs and centers.

UNINTENDED CONSEQUENCES

All bad outcomes of released products and services cannot be simply written off to unintended consequences. Commercial organizations have a responsibility to perform due diligence in minimizing the number of negative consequences and actively reducing what would otherwise be unforeseen negative outcomes. It is no longer acceptable that a corporate apology on social media excuses a company for rushing to market. This is not to say that companies must retreat to analysis paralysis and never ship anything that has some element of risk or that the threat of competition is not real. The purpose of this book is to enlist the power of the public to aid your organization in this mission, but there need to be channels and platforms for Citizen Futurists to do just that.

BUILD A BRIDGE FOR CITIZEN FUTURISTS

For organizations, foresight is important, but it is just as important that society be a part of the conversation. According to Metzl, the proof case for this was the introduction of genetically modified organisms (food); "Even though GMO was well planned, it was not reacted to well because people weren't part of the conversation."[290]

Today, corporations are making decisions about technological products and services that have far-reaching impacts on consumers. There is increasing awareness of the need to include the public—a broader and more diverse audience—into the R&D decision-making process. Advances in bioengineering, artificial intelligence, quantum computing, environmental sciences, and agriculture will be far more reaching in their impacts on humankind than innovation in our recent past. Many of these advancements pose ethical and moral situations that will undoubtedly be viewed both good and bad across the ideologies of our global community. In a recent Clubhouse room for AI, I asked the stage for any examples of how their organizations are taking input from the public seriously; after a long silence, one finally acknowledged that it is not happening, but that it should be.

The investment and control of Research and Development transitioned from government and universities to commercial entities around the turn of the century, leaving a vacuum of decision-making that involves society.[291] The consensus model had been used to some effect until then; over a couple of weekends, a selection of the general public would get to hear from technical experts and engage in discussions

---

290 Jamie Metzl, "Joe Rogan Experience #1294—Jamie Metzl," interview by Joe Rogan, *The Joe Rogan Experience*. May 10, 2019, audio, 2:29:00.
291 Chopyak, Jill, Peter and Levesque, "Public Participation in Science and Technology Decision Making: Trends for the Future," *Technology in Society* 24, no. 1-2 (2002):155-166.

around questions, issues, and concerns, as well as key considerations for public education, policymaking, and so forth.

Public participation includes all aspects of identifying problems and opportunities, developing alternatives, and making decisions. It uses tools and techniques that are common to a number of dispute resolution and communications fields. If you decide to experiment or ramp up your civic engagement efforts for these big and important conversations, consider using a public engagement specialist. If you don't have one in-house, consult, support, or partner with one of several nonprofit organizations such as NCDD, IAP2, The Loka Institute, or ECAST.

National Coalition for Dialogue & Deliberation (NCDD) is a network of innovators who bring people together across divides to discuss, decide, and take action together effectively on today's toughest issues. NCDD serves as a gathering place, a resource center, a news source, and a facilitative leader for this vital community of practice. International Association for Public Participation (IAP2) views public participation as any process that involves the public in problem-solving or decision making and uses public input to make decisions. The Loka Institute of Science and Technology, the tagline for which is "by and for the people," tracks citizen-based deliberative consensus conferences worldwide. Expert & Citizen Assessment of Science & Technology (ECAST)—Distributed Network of Institutions for Peer-to-Peer Public Deliberation is a community of academic research, informal science education, and citizen science programs that provide non-partisan policy analysis and public engagement.

RESPONSIBLE RESEARCH AND INNOVATION

Corporate social responsibility has been a topic area of research and management theory for decades. A more recent development in the same vein is responsible research and innovation (RRI), introduced in 2009 by Robinson through an analysis of policy concepts for nanotechnology development.[292] According to Martinuzzi, Block, Brem, Stahl, and Schönherr, RRI presents an opportunity to address two primary issues that have come up with industry-driven innovation.[293]

- The sustained competitive pressure to innovate
- The increasing public pressure for industry to create social value (not just economic growth)

The tension between these two factors leads to escalation when they come into conflict.[294] Recognizing this, the approach of RRI has been embraced by the European Union, having been adopted as a new policy concept in 2013 and is included in the EU Horizon 2020 Framework Programme for Research and Innovation.[295]

The RRI framework includes six pillars: ethics, gender equality, governance, open access, public engagement, and science

---

292 Lukasz Nazarko, "Responsible Research and Innovation—a Conceptual Contribution to Theory and Practice of Technology Management," *Business: Theory and Practice* 20, (August 2019):342-51.
293 André Martinuzzi, Vincent Blok, Alexander Brem, Bernd Stahl, Norma Schönherr, "Responsible Research and Innovation in Industry—Challenges, Insights and Perspectives," *Sustainability* 10, no. 3. (2018): 702.
294 Ibid.
295 Lukasz Nazarko, "Responsible Research and Innovation—a Conceptual Contribution to Theory and Practice of Technology Management."

education.[296] RRI has garnered a lot of attention, particularly from European researchers, as there have been research funds made available for the pursuit of innovation utilizing the RRI framework.

REINING IN CONSEQUENCES
Tonn and Stiefel looked through the lens of consequences—anticipated intended consequences (AIC), anticipated unintended consequences (AUC), and unanticipated unintended consequences (UUC).[297] In their research, which aimed to create a foresight framework for consequences, they evaluated the framework against historical advancements. These included social media platforms, biometrics for security, antidepressants' impact on the environment, genetically modified bioluminescent plants, and brain pacemakers.[298] Each of these innovations had an authentic purpose for good; however, each also came with undesirable consequences. In a world where public pressure is often required to incentivize organizations and governments to do the right thing, this evidence suggests that the world of innovation should be more transparent and inclusive.

BEYOND THE EARLY ADOPTERS
Everyone in business school is taught to cater to their target audience, so it makes perfect sense that companies in science

---

296 Ibid.
297 Bruce Edward Tonn and Dorian Stiefel, "Anticipating the Unanticipated-Unintended Consequences of Scientific and Technological Purposive Actions," *World Futures Review* 11, no. 1 (March 2019): 19–50.
298 Ibid.

and technology focus their outreach efforts on like-minded conferences. When the value of innovation is targeted at the general population, you must communicate with audiences broader than attendees of CES and SxSW. People who are not actively involved in these industries are most likely unaware of these innovations nor understand how the time horizon until their arrival is shortening. It can be argued that it is the duty of the innovation community to educate and involve others in the debates of our future. In a culture with many demands and distractions, it can be difficult to garner attention and engagement on policy-type issues. Modern methods for civic engagement on fundamental innovations are needed by public and private organizations.

By looking beyond innovators and early adopters, organizations can solicit the input of those late-adoption groups and get a sense of their behaviors and values. Consider the many product launches that seem to have missed the mark, either arriving too early, too late, or with the wrong value prop altogether—going back to Beta video and flashing forward to Microsoft Tablet PC, 3D TV, and Google Glasses. The geek-gadget new-tech-loving consumers will have a hard time seeing the future when the broader market won't adopt what they are playing with today. Foresight that isn't focused on technology, but looks at other factors, including consumer behaviors and societal trends, is better informed by looking beyond. To do this effectively, organizations must build up this skill in-house or look to work with a partner.

Uber and Lyft learned a tough lesson about working out of cycle from gig workers and policymakers, and the effects will flow to other gig-worker services. In February 2021, the

United Kingdom's Supreme Court ruled that Uber drivers qualify as workers and must be treated accordingly. The State of California had reached the same conclusion in the fall of 2020.[299]

So, you are ready to engage—but how? Research is emerging on just this question. Covered earlier in the book are two other ways to engage the public. Projects like MIT's Media Lab moral machine experiment or McGonigal's leveraged crowd-source input to inform research for innovation. Gamification platforms can be a great way for public entities to crowd-source public input. Hassan provides a theoretical framework for the gamification of civic engagement platforms that drew upon self-determination theory and democratic deliberation theory; it utilizes the common characteristics employed in gamification: motivational affordances, psychological outcomes, and behavioral outcomes.[300]

***

I close this chapter with a quote from the About page of the Expert & Citizen Assessment of Science & Technology website:

The perspectives, interests, and values of lay citizens are too often left out of scientific and technological debates. Scientists

---

[299] Natasha Bernal, "Uber has Lost in the Supreme Court. Here's What Happens Next," *Wired*, February 19, 2021; Irina Ivanova, "California Appeals Court Says Uber, Lyft Drivers are Employees, Not Contractors," *CBS News*, October 23, 2020.

[300] Lobna Hassan, "Governments Should Play Games: Towards a Framework for the Gamification of Civic Engagement Platforms." *Simulation and Gaming* 48, no. 2, (2017): 249-267.

and other experts decide how to frame and address important matters early on, frequently viewing them as purely technical questions. This upstream lack of transparency and inclusion damages the scientific enterprise's legitimacy and often misses issues of vital concern to citizens.... Changing this dynamic requires informing and deliberating with the otherwise-disengaged public early and often, providing decision support and diverse perspectives for the significant choices confronting society.[301]

How will you lead your organization to a broader conversation with the public, starting with Citizen Futurists?

---

301 "About," *Expert & Citizen Assessment of Science & Technology*, accessed March 1, 2021.

14

POLICY INFLUENCERS

Much of what has been shared throughout this book is probably not new to the policy concerned. The fact is policymakers, political strategists, and non-government organizations are immersed in the space of strategic planning, change, and civic engagement. Still, as we have seen, especially in recent times, there are issues with speed and prioritization of preparation, policy creation, and change readiness. The pandemic is only one recent albeit large example.

Texas started 2021 off with extreme weather, and its infrastructure was not ready. Unable to respond rapidly to challenges, Texas citizens were left in the dark cold without clean water for several days. The potential for these problems was identified after an investigation of similar events in 2011. Rinne shared with me how she spoke with many international government leaders who were not tracking major shifts in behaviors, such as the sharing economy bringing the arrival of services like Airbnb. Mayors would come to Rinne for guidance on regulating a service that they had never used nor realized was already being operated in their jurisdictions. As

Rinne said, there is nothing more dangerous than attempting to regulate that which you do not understand.

It is widely acknowledged that most nations were not sufficiently prepared for COIVD-19. As mentioned earlier, the Global Health Security Index warned, "National health security is fundamentally weak around the world. No country is fully prepared for epidemics or pandemics, and every country has important gaps to address."[302] That risk in your register marked low frequency but high impact must not be ignored; it needs to be framed and managed.

In 2018, Arndt Husar spoke at the UN's High-Level Political Forum (HLPF) on sustainable development:

There are new tools needed, to gather intelligence about the future, identify emerging strategic opportunities, measure cross-sectional impact of policies, enhance our ability to spot risks and identify opportunities, increase our ability to anticipate and adapt, and engage unusual suspects/new change agents. [...] [Be] like surfers to actually navigate the change by riding on top of a wave not being hit by it and basically not being blown across the ocean like a sailing boat wherever the wind takes them but to really navigate this change.[303]

Some public leaders are aware of the need. The Department of Defense Innovation Unit exists but needs to move faster, according to Michael Brown, Unit Director. According to

---

302 Cameron, Elizabeth E., ed., Jennifer B. Nuzzo, ed., Jessica A. Bell, ed. "2019 Global Health Security Index." *Global Health Security Index.*

303 "The Use of Strategic Foresight for Adaptive and Future-Ready SDG Strategies," UNDP Global Centre for Public Service Excellence.

Brown, the now-five-year-old DIU has been successful since former Defense Secretary Ash Carter stood it up but needs to move faster.[304] One way to move faster is to use foresight to see what is coming.

Moving slowly is but one problem. Many of the problems facing us today have seen no plans for solving, despite related advancements and solutions. Because there is often no clear owner because the private sector is not incented to solve the problem, and public entities don't have the resources. Two examples that Bet-David discussed with Holman included forest management problems in California and increasing hurricane intensity.[305] While both problems have plausible mitigations or perhaps even solutions, no entity has the resources, capabilities, and incentive to tackle them. Unless something changes, the only way to fix all these problems is to work harder to directly educate and involve the public—in more than urban planning.

ENGAGING THE PUBLIC

Beat Habbeger reports in the *Futures Journal* February 2010 edition that with regard to civic engagement:

The two distinct ways in which it contributes to public policy-making: on the one hand, it informs policy by providing more systematic knowledge about relevant trends and developments

---

304 Terri Moon Cronck, "DOD Innovation Speed Must Increase to Modernize," *DOD News*, August 7, 2020.
305 Pablos Holman, "Futurist & Hacker Reveals How to Solve World's Biggest Problems," interview by Patrick Bet-David, *Valuetainment*, October 23, 2020, video, 1:17:41.

in an organization's environments; on the other hand, it acts as a driver of reflexive mutual social learning processes among policymakers that stimulate the generation of common public policy visions.[306]

Modern methods for civic engagement are needed by public organizations. Public organizations must design engagement programs for the public with regard to R&D for technological innovations. "Public policy requires public support, which in turn implies a need to enable the public not just to understand policy but also to be engaged in its development. Where complex science and technology issues are involved in policy-making, this takes time, so it is important to identify emerging issues of this type and prepare engagement plans."[307]

Corporate Social Responsibility has been a topic area of research and management theory for decades. A more recent development in the same vein is Responsible Research and Innovation (RRI), introduced in 2009 by Robinson through an analysis of policy concepts for nanotechnology development (Nazarko, 2019).[308] According to Martinuzzi, Block, Brm, Stahl, and Schonherr, RRI presents an opportunity to

---

306 Beat Habegger, "Strategic Foresight in Public Policy: Reviewing the Experiences of the UK, Singapore, and the Netherlands, *Futures* 42, no. 1 (February 2010): 49-58.
307 Miles Parker et al., "Identifying the Science and Technology Dimensions of Emerging Public Policy Issues Through Horizon Scanning," *PloS One* 9, no. 5 (May 20, 2014).
308 Lucasz Nazarko. "Responsible Research and Innovation—A Conceptual Contribution to Theory and Practice of Technology Management." *Business: Theory and Practice* 20 (2019), 342-351.

address two primary issues that have come up with industry-driven innovation:[309]

- The sustained competitive pressure to innovate
- The increasing public pressure for industry to create social value (not just economic growth)

The tension between these two factors leads to escalation when they come into conflict.[310] Recognizing this, the approach of RRI has been embraced by the European Union, having been adopted as a new policy concept in 2013 and is included in the EU Horizon 2020 Framework Programme for Research and Innovation.[311] The literature reviewed thus far does not find an application of RRI in the United States civic environment.

The RRI framework includes six pillars: ethics, gender equality, governance, open access, public engagement, and science education.[312] RRI has garnered a lot of attention, particularly from European researchers, as there have been research funds made available for the pursuit of innovation utilizing the RRI framework. There has been an increasing number of articles on the topic. The research on RRI, along with additional related works, are pulled in to explore definitions,

---

309 Andre Martinuzzi, Vincent Blok, Alexander Brem, Bernd Stahl, Norma Schonherr, "Responsible Research and Innovation in Industry—Challenges, Insights and Perspectives," *Sustainability (Switzerland)* 10, no. 3, (2018): 1–10.
310 Ibid.
311 Lucasz Nazarko, "Responsible Research and Innovation—A Conceptual Contribution to Theory and Practice of Technology Management."
312 Ibid.

history, and opportunities as applied to the primary research area to answer the questions above.

There is a clear call for treating the public as a stakeholder and key external actor in the RRI process.[313]

This need is called out explicitly in the RRI literature, either as external actors or as civil society outright. Ceicyte and Petraite considered that with the case of the employee, they act both as an internal actor, influenced by organization ethics and norms, as well as their own individual values and morals. These researchers evaluated the entire network of responsibility to assess the perspective of the firm with regard to RRI.[314]

The tenets of the RRI framework include diversity, anticipatory, openness—including transparency and integrity, and responsiveness.[315] These must be based on normative values like the United Nations Sustainable Development Goals;

---

313 Jolita Ceicyte and Monika Petraite, "Networked Responsibility Approach for Responsible Innovation: Perspective of the Firm," *Sustainability* 10, no. 6, (March 18, 2018): 1720; Sara H. Wilford, "First Line Steps in Requirements Identification for Guidelines Development in Responsible Research and Innovation (RRI)," *Systemic Practice and Action Research* 31, (January 25, 2018): 539-556; Bruce Edward Tonn and Dorian Stiefel, "Anticipating the Unanticipated-Unintended Consequences of Scientific and Technological Purposive Actions," *World Futures Review* 11, no. 1, (August 1, 2018): 19–50.

314 Jolita Ceicyte and Monika Petraite, "Networked Responsibility Approach for Responsible Innovation: Perspective of the Firm."

315 Richard Owen, Phil Macnaghten, Jack Stilgoe, Responsible Research and Innovation: From Science in Society to Science for Society, with Society, *Science and Public Policy* 39, no. 6 (December 2012): 751–760. https://doi.org/10.1093/scipol/scs093.

because norms vary among cultures, a diverse set of voices must be included in the process—including the public.

Creating channels of engagement for the community requires an understanding of the drivers of creating interest in such engagement and supporting research on the engagement methods that prove most effective for innovation in science and technology. There is evidence of the ancillary importance of civic engagement:

Citizens' sense of responsibility to their community and to their nation is becoming a topic of growing concern. Recent research indicates that citizens of the United States and many other nations have become increasingly disconnected from their fellow community members, and when this connection is lost, individuals begin to suffer. They experience poorer health, achieve lower academic and employment success, and are at risk for the development of a host of social problems. On a broader level, states and countries whose citizens feel detached from their communities show higher levels of crime, a greater incidence of disease, and even higher mortality rates.[316]

Engagement of the public has been beneficial; there have been successful engagements between scientists and non-scientists in research, primarily in the areas of environmental issues and health.[317] Williams conducted an experiment with electronic public participation that focused on the health risk

---

316 S. Mark Pancer, The Psychology of Citizenship and Civic Engagement, (Oxford: Oxford University Press, 2014).
317 Christopher Kullenberg and Dick Kasperowski, "What Is Citizen Science?—A Scientometric Meta-Analysis," *PLoS One* 11, no. 1 (January 2016).

posed by mobile telephones.[318] Parker, et al, analyzed and identified key dimensions of public policy issues that relate to science and technology.[319] Chopyak and Levesque provided an inventory of methods used around the world that address the shift of attitudes around science and provide citizens with an opportunity to participate in science and technology decision-making processes.[320]

There are examples to be found for engaging the public in a meaningful way, typically in response to the Open Government Directive established under Obama. The directive instructed agencies to take immediate, specific steps to open their doors and data to the American people.[321] The Obama Administration left office with mixed results in executing this directive, and efforts slowed or halted under the Trump administration.[322] Still, many have pushed forward given the value of the intent. Jerome H. Powell, Chair of the Board of Governors for the Federal Reserve System, had this to say about the "Fed Listens" public engagement events that they held in 2019: "[They] were just really striking—that conference there were two panels of people from low- and

---

318 Simon N. Williams, "A Twenty-First Century Citizens' POLIS: Introducing a Democratic Experiment in Electronic Citizen Participation in Science and Technology Decision-Making." *Public Understanding of Science* 19, no. 5 (September 2010): 528–44.
319 Miles Parker et al., "Identifying the Science and Technology Dimensions of Emerging Public Policy Issues Through Horizon Scanning."
320 Jill Chopyak and Peter Levesque. "Public Participation in Science and Technology Decision Making: Trends for the Future." *Technology in Society* 25 (2002): 155-166.
321 Peter R. Orszag, "Open Government Directive," The White House, December 8, 2009 (memorandum), accessed February 21, 2021.
322 Briana Williams, "Under Trump, US Government Moves from /Open to /Closed," Sunlight Foundation, January 24, 2018.

moderate-income communities who spoke about the economy in their lives. It was the highlight of that conference. To hear from them on what a tight labor market in their community means is something we won't forget."[323] The US Nuclear Regulatory Commission provides public access to information and includes a public meeting schedule.[324]

ENLISTING HELP

Public entities don't have to go it alone. Engage the public with a partner. McGonigal has designed gamified experiences for organizations like Microsoft, McDonald's, the American Heart Association, the World Bank Institute, the Oprah Winfrey Network, and many others. One platform experience she highlights on her website is an effort to crowdsource ideas for how to advise the president for the following scenario:

A widespread contamination has triggered a neurological disease that is expected to infect as many as one hundred million people in the US. Government leaders have convened a panel to investigate ways to accelerate the pace of research and find treatments or cures for this disease before it strikes.[325]

For public engagement support, as recommended in the last chapter, consider using public engagement specialists like from the National Coalition for Dialogue & Deliberation (NCDD) and International Association for Public

---

323 Reuters, "Federal Reserve Chair Jerome Powell Discusses Monetary Policy," August 27, 2020, video, 58:38.
324 "The NRC Approach to Open Government," USNRC, accessed February 20, 2021.
325 Jane McGonical, "Games—Play Me," accessed February 19, 2021.

Participation (IAP2). NCDD is a network of innovators who bring people together across divides to discuss, decide, and act together effectively on today's toughest issues. NCDD serves as a gathering place, a resource center, a news source, and a facilitative leader for this vital community of practice. IAP2 views public participation as any process that involves the public in problem-solving or decision making and uses public input to make decisions.

Public participation includes all aspects of identifying problems and opportunities, developing alternatives, and making decisions. It uses tools and techniques common to a number of dispute resolution and communications fields. As noted in Chapter 12, there are academic centers finding ways to connect audiences for broad inclusion, such as Arizona State University's Consortium for Science, Policy, and Outcomes.

***

Policymakers have expansive, complex jobs and millions of critics. I respect anyone willing to pursue public service as a career. What may make the job a little easier is to be flexible in thinking, use foresight tools, and engage a broad audience in the process. There are many ways to approach it, from the transparency in the Open Government Initiative to hearing stories directly from constituents as in the Fed Listens events. There can be public salons, consensus forums, workshops, and so many more options. And when the future is pressing enough, "the unthinkable becomes thinkable, as with COVID," says Leonhard.[326]

How will you pursue the full fidelity of open government?

---

326 *Gerd Leonhard*, "Ten Essential Future Foresights for a Post Corona World: A Covid-19 Virtual Keynote by Gerd Leonhard," June 22, 2020, video, 47:48.

CONCLUSION

Congratulations! You have taken another—or perhaps your first—step toward thinking about the future differently and with more intention than ever before. Now you can begin to start the dialogue in your community about a topic of interest or simply leveling up the opportunity to take agency in your future. You know now there is not one future—there are many, and no one can predict it. They can only look at signals and patterns to identify what may happen. Encourage or even challenge your families and friends to begin this journey with you.

We defined key terminology: citizen futurism and futures thinking. You learned how to build your futures-thinking muscles through both visualization and critical thinking. We looked at the stories and attributes of professional futurists and identified some of the human instincts that inhibit our futures thinking. You learned about how to look around you and behind you to paint pictures of the future. We looked at key areas of innovation like nuclear technology, bioengineering, climate change, and artificial intelligence. You pondered your biases and whether you tend to think more optimistically or tend to get into the dark futures. You learned that futures looking happens every day, in everything you do—and how it can be a focus of your planning. We built scenarios and tested and prioritized them based on framing, uncertainty, and perceived consequences. Finally, you looked at the many opportunities to act.

The biggest takeaway I want you to have is that you have agency. You can influence the future, whether through individual decisions or by becoming a global activist.

The book is jam-packed with information, so take time to revisit sections of particular interest and refer back to it as you attempt various activities of futures thinking. Look for the additional resources that will become available online after the launch of the book.

Be a bridge maker—look, think, and act.

RESOURCES

Feed your brain and build your futures literacy with the following resources, including bridgemakersbook.com and many from people mentioned in this book:

Tayo Adesanya: His consumer products business, backpacks that offer charging capabilities, supports the STEM programming by Adesanya: agbaralife.com.

Nikolas Badminton: Learn more about Badminton on his site, nikolasbadminton.com, and listen to his podcast *Exponential Minds*. He is an active contributor to futurist.com. He also recommends the community found at reddit.com/r/Futurology. Badminton wrote the opening chapter for the book *The Future Starts Now: Expert Insights into the Future of Business, Technology and Society*.

Joe Farro: Check out Farro's adventures on his YouTube channel, GeekToolKit. He can also be found on Twitter @geektoolkit1 and Instagram at @geektoolkit.

Pablos Holman: Holman launched his *Jetpack for the Mind* podcast this year. You can learn more about him at pablosspeaks.com.

Anab Jain: Learn more about SuperFlux at superflux.in.

Jane McGonigal: Learn more about McGonigal at janemcgonigal.com, or check out her course for Institute for the Future on Coursera!

Jamie Metzl: Hear more from Metzl at jamiemetzl.com, and check out his books including *Hacking Darwin*.

April Rinne: Learn more at aprilrinne.com as well as the site for her book, fluxmindset.com. You can find her book *Flux: 8 Superpowers for Thriving in Constant Change* on Amazon.

Ryan O' Shea: Check out the Future Grind podcast and learn more at futuregrind.org or his #IAmTranhumanism initiatives at iamtranshuman.org. He also recommends the "non-obvious" trends episodes from the podcast convinceandconvert.com.

Cecily Sommers: Find Sommers' book *Think Like a Futurist* on Amazon, and look for more tools and resources on her site cecilysommers.com.

Bronwyn Williams: Check out Williams' site at whatthefuturenow.com or agency fluxtrends.com. She also collaborated with others like Badminton to create the book *The Future Starts Now: Expert Insights into the Future of Business, Technology and Society*.

***

A few sources I include in my feeds:

Exponential View from Azeem Azhar

Freakonomics podcast

Futurism.com

MIT Technology Review

NEO.LIFE from Jane Metcalfe

Word Economic Forum

Here are just a few sources of annual trends reports that I read:

Accenture

Fjord Design and Innovation

Flux Trends

Frog Design

Future Today Institute

GfK

Mary Meeker

McKinsey

Nikolas Badminton

PSFK

Ray Kurzweil

World Economic Forum

ACKNOWLEDGMENTS

First, I acknowledge the strength, energy, and light sourced from my spiritual journey over the years, my ultimate bridge maker, especially when my own perceived future has created anxiety.

There may be one name on the cover, but dozens of names are behind the creation.

My heartfelt gratitude to the Book Creators and New Degree Press families, with the many talented folks helping hundreds of authors bring their stories and knowledge to the world, especially Eric Koester, founder of the Book Creators program, who extended the invitation to this crazy journey; my development editor Michael Butler; my acquiring editor Jen Wichman; my marketing and revisions editor Mozelle Jordan; Alexander Pavlovich, my layout editor; and their assorted wranglers. Each of you played a vital role in shaping this work—thank you.

Thank you to Teaque Lenahan for reviewing and providing feedback on key sections.

Particularly as an unknown and first-time author, it is with my deepest gratitude to those who shared some of their precious time with me and lent their words of wisdom and brilliant insights to shape and lift the messages in this book: Adetayo Adesanya, Curt Aumiller, Gene Becker, Nikolas Badminton, Pablos Holman, Ryan O'Shea, April Rinne, Cecily Sommers, and Bronwyn Williams.

Special thanks to Jamie Metzl, a big inspiration for this book who offered me his support even though he could not take time to speak. And while the secondary sources in general are many, I would like to specifically call out the brilliance of Amy Webb (TFTI), Anab Jain (Superflux), Jane McGonigal (IFTF), Gerd Leonhard, and Stuart Candy (Carnegie Mellon University).

Now, to acknowledge those who truly humbled me, the *123 Indiegogo campaign backers* who had the faith to honor this project without having read a single word. I am grateful for each and every one of you for your trust and support in this project—from the bottom of my heart, thank you for being a bridge maker. Below are all who elected to be named as backers:

Author Champion

Jake Zukowski: "I'm proud of you. Writing a book takes some guts." Quick and substantial support is amazing, especially when it comes from someone so authentically bold and grounded (yet adventurous), as he. An avid reader and frequent *Goodreads* reviewer, Jake's support for this new author conveys a vote of confidence (which I gratefully tapped into as I labored to cross the finish line). Thank you, Jake, for your support and inspiration, not only in this effort but since and every day during our time at Fjord.

Sponsored a Classroom

Munawar Ahmed: It was a quick and easy decision to sponsor for Ahmed. Before her many years of work helping clients and agencies bring innovation and rigor to their practice, Ahmed was a middle school teacher. From 1998–2000, she chaired the science department at John Adams Middle School in South Central LA. She taught eighth grade science and imbued hope and discipline in her 180 students. She was lauded as one the most charismatic teachers to walk into the school in the last decade and did a complete overhaul of the science program, replenished laboratory materials, winning $112,000 in educational grant monies. Munawar, thank you, and I cannot wait to take this into a classroom with you!

Acknowledgments

Amber Marie McFarland
Andrew Geleff[M]
Andy Pennell
Antti Routto[M]
Arne Gaenz[M]
Avery Avecilla-Datol[T]
Benjamin Allen[T]
Bernard Schultz[T]
Bill Stevenson[M]
Bill/Becky Rodenbeck[M]
Bret Grinslade[T]

Carin Coty
Carol Whisenant
Chintan Bakshi
Dan Kim
Dana Grau
Dean Wills[E]
Deanna Kennedy[E]
Debra Trappen
Doug Loiler
Dwipal Desai[T]
Elida Cruz[T]
Eric Koester
Eric VanThorre
Eric Veal[T]
Eric Watt
Ernie Booth
Eugene Becker[M]
Evelyn Stewart
Florian Dusch
Forest W Gouin
Garth Lewis
Glenn Noyama
Grace Bentson
Jacob Fordham[E]
James Hicks
Jay Ewell
Jeff Cann[M]
Jennifer Gaona
Jerry D Higgins
John Anderson Cunningham
John Bass
Jon Thompson

Jordan Kilpatric
Joseph Farro[T]
Joyann Troutman
Karin Meier
Kelly Damron
Laura Kogut
Lianne Morgan[M]
Lily Xu
Liz Blaszczak
Liz Hanson[M]
Lori Marshall[T]
Luis Cabrera
Martha Cotton
Mathieu Albrand
Michael Day
Mike Gadow[M]
Nathan Rodenbeck
Nik Bhattacharya
Panos Panay[M]
Patricia Smith
Penny Ewell
Peter Hauge
Rachel Kobetz
Rich Gaona
Rico Mariani[M]
Robert E Clark[M]
Robert Levy
Rohitashwa Jain
Rosa Ramos
Keith Rowe[T]
Rusty Miller
Sandra Rodenbeck

Sarissa Marwitz[M]
Scott Failing
Shellie Mazzella
Steven Christopher Boswell[T]
Tanarra M. Schneider[M]
Tanner Sutton
Teri Smith[M]
Thomas Mueller
Todd Hendricks
Uday Shivaswamy
Veronica De la Pena
Wayne Suiter Matamoros
T—Also sponsored a teacher
M—Purchased multiple copies in advance
E—Educator Guide reviewer

Digital Backers:

Amy Ritz
Andy Polaine
Brian Evans
Callie Helen
Chris Clements
Daniel Fernandez
Ehud Paz
Gamage Viriththamulla
James Maki
Katya Tebeleva
Laura Escude
Martina Hiemstra
Matt Dobbin

Matthew P Lazear
Michell Thyng
Nathan Bushey
Swati Doshi
Tony Goodhew
Vince Thyng

BIBLIOGRAPHY

BOOK EPIGRAPH

Dromgoole, Will Allen. *Father: An Anthology of Verse*. (New York: EP Dutton & Company, 1931).

INTRODUCTION

Gibbons, John H. *Office of Technology Assessment: Computerized Manufacturing Automation*. Washington D.C.: Congressional Board of the 98th Congress, Library of Congress, OTA-CIT-235. April 1984. https://files.eric.ed.gov/fulltext/ED248355.pdf.

Merriam-Webster Dictionary Online. s.v. "futurist." Accessed February 16, 2021, http://www.merriam-webster.com/dictionary/futurist.

Schultz, Colin. "Some People See Their Future-Selves as Strangers." *Smithsonian Magazine,* October 29, 2012. https://www.smithsonianmag.com/smart-news/some-people-see-their-future-selves-as-strangers-98378412/.

Ted Archive. "Building bridges and connecting communities | Avery Bang." May 7, 2018. Video, 14:58. https://www.youtube.com/watch?v=6SroqQlK2g4.

Torooc. "A Robot in Every Home." Accessed March 23, 2021. https://www.torooc.com/.

United Nations Educational, Scientific and Cultural Organization. "Futures Literacy." Accessed February 16, 2021, https://en.unesco.org/futuresliteracy/about.

PART 1 EPIGRAPH

Orr, David W. *Earth in Mind: On Education, Environment, and the Human Prospect.* Washington D.C.: Island Press, 2004.

CHAPTER 1

Bersin, Josh, and Marco Zao-Sanders. "Boost Your Team's Data Literacy." *Harvard Business Review.* February 12, 2020. https://hbr.org/2020/02/boost-your-teams-data-literacy.

Briggs, Sara. "Why Visual Literacy is More Important than Ever and Five Ways to Cultivate It." *InformEd.* November 7, 2015. https://www.opencolleges.edu.au/informed/features/why-visual-literacy-is-more-important-than-ever-10-ways-to-cultivate-it/.

Brooks, Ashley. "Health Literacy: What is It and Why is It Important?" *Health and Sciences* (blog). *Rasmussen University.* November 18, 2019. https://www.rasmussen.edu/degrees/health-sciences/blog/importance-of-health-literacy/.

Byrnie, Faith. "Remembering Something That Never Happened." *Psychology Today.* July 26, 2013. https://www.psychologytoday.com/us/blog/brain-sense/201307/remembering-something-never-happened.

Concern Worldwide. "COVID-19 is a Humanitarian Crisis." Accessed February 16, 2021. https://www.concernusa.org/our-approach/emergency-response/covid-response/.

Diamond, Jared. *Collapse: How Societies Choose to Fail or Succeed.* (New York: Penguin Books, 2011).

Ferrari, Joseph. "Psychology of Procrastination." American Psychological Association. 2010. https://www.apa.org/news/press/releases/2010/04/procrastination.

Giovetti, Olivia. "6 Benefits of Literacy in the Fight Against Poverty." *Concern Worldwide*. August 27, 2020. Accessed March 10, 2021. https://www.concernusa.org/story/benefits-of-literacy-against-poverty/.

Itkowitz, Colby. "Harvard Professor: 'It is Natural and Normal to be Physically Lazy'." *The Sydney Morning Herald*. September 16, 2016. https://www.smh.com.au/lifestyle/harvard-professor-it-is-natural-and-normal-to-be-physically-lazy-20160916-grhipc.html.

Koomen, Rebecca, Sebastian Grueneisen, and Esther Herrmann. "Children Delay Gratification for Cooperative Ends." *Psychological Science* 31, no. 2 (February 2020): 139–48. https://doi.org/10.1177/0956797619894205.

Merriam-Webster Dictionary Online. s.v. "literate." Accessed February 16, 2021, https://www.merriam-webster.com/dictionary/literate#h1.

Mitchell, Jason P., Jessica Schirmer, Daniel L Ames, and Daniel T Gilbert. "Medial Prefrontal Cortex Predicts Intertemporal Choice." *Journal of cognitive neuroscience* 23, no. 4 (2011): 857-66. doi:10.1162/jocn.2010.21479.

Mischel, W., E. B. Ebbesen, A.R. Zeiss. "Cognitive and Attentional Mechanisms in Delay of Gratification." *Journal of Personality and Social Psychology* 21 (1972):204-218.

Neuroscience News. "Mental Rehearsal Prepares Our Brains for Real World Actions." February 16, 2018. https://neurosciencenews.com/mental-rehearsal-action-8505/.

President's Advisory Council on Financial Literacy. *2008 Report to the President*. (Washington D.C.: The Department of the Treasury, 2008). Accessed on February 16, 2021. https://www.

treasury.gov/resource-center/financial-education/Documents/PACFL_ANNUAL_REPORT_1-16-09.pdf.

Ratzan, Scott C. "Vaccine Literacy, a Crucial Healthcare Innovation." *Harvard Business Review,* February 28, 2011. https://hbr.org/2011/02/vaccine-literacy-a-crucial-hea.

Solly, Meilan. "Why Delayed Gratification in the Marshmallow Test Doesn't Equal Success." *Smithsonian Magazine,* June 5, 2018. https://www.smithsonianmag.com/smart-news/new-research-marshmallow-test-suggests-delayed-gratification-doesnt-equal-success-180969234/.

Steenbarger, Brett. "Tapping the Power of Mental Rehearsal." *Forbes.* February 17, 2018. https://www.forbes.com/sites/brettsteenbarger/2018/02/17/tapping-the-power-of-mental-rehearsal/?sh=3a5ea18866f0.

SxSW. "Amy Webb's Emerging Tech Trends for 2020." May 6, 2020. Video, 5:02. https://www.youtube.com/watch?v=uoD-5M66p3yU.

Taylor, Jim. "Is Our Survival Instinct Failing Us?" *Psychology Today.* June 12, 2012. https://www.psychologytoday.com/us/blog/the-power-prime/201206/is-our-survival-instinct-failing-us.

Taylor, Jim. "Sport Imagery: Athletes' Most Powerful Mental Tool—Are You Using Mental Imagery to Maximize Your Sports Performances?" *Psychology Today.* November 6, 2012. https://www.psychologytoday.com/us/blog/the-power-prime/201211/sport-imagery-athletes-most-powerful-mental-tool.

United Nations Educational, Scientific and Cultural Organization. "Futures Literacy." Accessed February 16, 2021. https://en.unesco.org/futuresliteracy/about.

University of Rochester. "The Marshmallow Study Revisited." October 11, 2012. http://www.rochester.edu/news/show.php?id=4622.

Vyas, Saurabh, Nir Evan-Chen, Sergey D. Stavisky, Stephen I. Ryu, Paul Nuyujukian and Krishna V. Shenoy. "Neural Population Dynamics Underlying Motor Learning Transfer." *Neuron*, 97, no. 5. (March 07, 2018): 1177-1186. https://www.cell.com/neuron/fulltext/S0896-6273(18)30065-5#articleInformation.

Wallace, Lauren, Nicholas Raison, Faisal Ghumman, Aidan Moran, Prokar Dasgupta, Kamran Ahmed. "Cognitive Training: How Can It Be Adapted for Surgical Education?" *The Surgeon* 15, no. 4 (2017): 231-239. https://doi.org/10.1016/j.surge.2016.08.003.

World Economic Forum. "New Vision for Education." March 2016. http://www3.weforum.org/docs/WEF_New_Vision_for_Education.pdf.

CHAPTER 2

APS. "Physicists Coalition for Nuclear Threat Reduction." Accessed February 17, 2021. https://aps.org/policy/nuclear/.

BBC. "A Brief History of Climate Change." September 20, 2013. https://www.bbc.com/news/science-environment-15874560.

Bettwy, Mike. "A Season in the Life of the Antarctic Ozone Hole: A Quarter Century of Satellite Measurements by TOMS." NASA, December 8, 2003. https://www.nasa.gov/vision/earth/lookingatearth/25TOMSAGU.html.

Encyclopædia Britannica Online, s.v. "Lisa Meitner." Accessed February 20, 2021, https://www.britannica.com/biography/Lise-Meitner.

Bulkey, Kate. "The Rise of Citizen Journalism." *The Guardian,* June 10, 2012. https://www.theguardian.com/media/2012/jun/11/rise-of-citizen-journalism.

Caldera, Camille. "Fact check: White House Didn't Fire Pandemic Response Unit When It was Disbanded in 2018." *USA Today,* September 10, 2020. https://www.usatoday.com/story/news/

factcheck/2020/09/10/fact-check-white-house-didnt-fire-pandemic-response-2018/3437356001/.

Cameron, Elizabeth E., ed., Jennifer B. Nuzzo, ed., Jessica A. Bell, ed. "2019 Global Health Security Index." Global Health Security Index. https://www.ghsindex.org/wp-content/uploads/2020/04/2019-Global-Health-Security-Index.pdf.

Centers for Disease Control and Prevention. "Our History—Our Story." Last updated December 4, 2018. https://www.cdc.gov/about/history/index.html.

Clifford, Catherine. "Bill Gates: How the Coronavirus Pandemic can Help the World Solve Climate Change." *CNBC*, March 31, 2020. https://www.cnbc.com/2020/03/31/bill-gates-how-covid-19-pandemic-can-help-world-solve-climate-change.html.

CNN. "President Trump Halts Funding to World Health Organization." April 14, 2020. Video, 7:33. https://www.youtube.com/watch?v=JjRMQk8yvDI.

Cooper, Katherine. "Wicked problems: What are They, and Why are They of Interest to NNSI Researchers?" *The Network for Nonprofit and Social Impact,* 2017. https://nnsi.northwestern.edu/wicked-problems-what-are-they-and-why-are-they-of-interest-to-nnsi-researchers/.

Cox, Kate. "Police Can Get Your Ring Doorbell Footage Without a Warrant, Report Says." *Ars Technica,* August 6, 2019. https://arstechnica.com/tech-policy/2019/08/police-can-get-your-ring-doorbell-footage-without-a-warrant-report-says/.

Dickinson College Digital Museum. "Showing Off: Scientific Lecturing in the 19th Century." Accessed on February 17, 2021. http://dh.dickinson.edu/digitalmuseum/exhibit-artifact/making-the-invisible-visible/showing-scientific-lecturing-19th-century.

Ducharme, Jamie. "World Health Organization Declares COVID-19 a 'Pandemic.' Here's What That Means." *Time*, March 11,

2020. https://time.com/5791661/who-coronavirus-pandemic-declaration/.

The Economist. "And Not a Drop to Drink a Cyber-attack on an American Water Plant Rattles Nerves." February 9, 2021. https://www.economist.com/united-states/2021/02/09/a-cyber-attack-on-an-american-water-plant-rattles-nerves.

European Centre for Disease Prevention and Control. "ECDC's Mission." Accessed February 18, 2021. https://www.ecdc.europa.eu/en/about-uswhat-we-do/ecdcs-mission.

Frick, Laurie. "Works." Accessed March 2, 2012. https://www.lauriefrick.com/works.

Gramling, Carolyn. "Wildfires, Heat Waves and Hurricanes Broke All Kinds of Records in 2020." *Science News,* December 21, 2020. https://www.sciencenews.org/article/climate-change-wildfires-heat-waves-hurricanes-records-2020.

History Channel. "Climate Change History." Last modified November 20, 2020. https://www.history.com/topics/natural-disasters-and-environment/history-of-climate-change.

Jain, Anab. "Why We Need to Imagine Different Futures." Filmed April 2017 in Vancouver, B.C. TED video, 14:31. https://www.ted.com/talks/anab_jain_why_we_need_to_imagine_different_futures.

Long, Bradon. "Record-setting Hurricane Season Continues as We Enter Greek Alphabet for Only the Second Time Ever." *Fox43 News,* September 21, 2020. https://www.fox43.com/article/weather/record-setting-hurricane-season-continues-greek-alphabet/521-c4ba5eca-09ec-4792-af9f-b80c1ad5d1db.

ITOPF. "Oil Tanker Spill Statistics 2020." Accessed February 17, 2021. https://www.itopf.org/knowledge-resources/data-statistics/statistics/.

McKie, Robin. "Climategate 10 Years On: What Lessons Have We :earned?" *The Observer,* November 9, 2019. https://www.

theguardian.com/theobserver/2019/nov/09/climategate-10-years-on-what-lessons-have-we-learned.

McNeil Jr., Donald G. "Scientists Were Hunting for the Next Ebola. Now the U.S. Has Cut Off Their Funding." *New York Times*, October 25, 2019. https://www.nytimes.com/2019/10/25/health/predict-usaid-viruses.html.

Mecklin, John, ed. "This is Your COVID Wake-up Call: It is 100 Seconds to Midnight." *Atomic Bulletin of Scientists*. Accessed February 17, 2021. https://thebulletin.org/doomsday-clock/current-time/.

Mecklin, John, ed. "Closer Than Ever: It is 100 Seconds to Midnight." *Atomic Bulletin of Scientists*. Accessed February 17, 2021. https://thebulletin.org/doomsday-clock/2020-doomsday-clock-statement/.

Morrisette, Paul M. "The Evolution of Policy Responses to Stratospheric Ozone Depletion." *Natural Resources Journal* 29, no 3 (Summer 1989):793-820. https://digitalrepository.unm.edu/nrj/vol29/iss3/9.

"This Month in Physics History." *APS News,* May 2007, 16, no. 5. Accessed February 17, 2021, https://aps.org/publications/apsnews/200705/physicshistory.cfm.

"This Month in Physics History." *APS News*, December 2007, Vol. 16, No. 11. Accessed February 17, 2021, https://www.aps.org/publications/apsnews/200712/physicshistory.cfm.

NASA. "2020 Tied for Warmest Year on Record, NASA Analysis Shows." January 14, 2021. https://climate.nasa.gov/news/3061/2020-tied-for-warmest-year-on-record-nasa-analysis-shows/.

Nesvizhevsky, Valery and Jacques Villain. "The Discovery of the Neutron and Its Consequences (1930–1940)." *Comptes Rendus Physique* 18, nos. 9–10, (November-December, 2017): 592-600. https://doi.org/10.1016/j.crhy.2017.11.001.

Newton, Casey. "How Extremism Came to Thrive on YouTube." *The Verge,* April 3, 2019. https://www.theverge.com/interface/2019/4/3/18293293/youtube-extremism-criticism-bloomberg.

Peterson, Thomas C., William M. Connolley, and John Fleck. "The Myth of the 1970s Global Cooling Scientific Consensus." *American Meteorological Society,* February 8, 2008. DOI:10.1175/2008BAMS2370.1.

Pinker, Steven. *Enlightenment Now.* New York: Penguin Random House, 2018.

Resse, Byron. *Infinite Progress.* Austin: Green Leaf Book Group Press, 2012.

Rich, Nathaniel. "How Climate Change Became a Partisan Issue." NPR, April 8, 2019. https://www.npr.org/2019/04/08/711067055/how-climate-change-became-a-partisan-issue.

Roser, Max, and Estaban Ortiz-Ospina. "Historical Poverty Around the World." Our World in Data, last updated in 2019. https://ourworldindata.org/extreme-poverty#historical-poverty-around-the-world.

Rosling, Hans. *Factfulness.* New York: Flatiron Books, 2018.

Stoller-Conrad, Jessica. "Tree Rings Provide Snapshots of Earth's Past Climate." NASA, January 25, 2017. https://climate.nasa.gov/news/2540/tree-rings-provide-snapshots-of-earths-past-climate/.

Stupples, David. "What is Information Warfare?" World Economic Forum, December 3, 2015. https://www.weforum.org/agenda/2015/12/what-is-information-warfare.

Swift, John. "The Soviet-American Arms Race." *History in Review* 63, March 2009. https://www.historytoday.com/archive/soviet-american-arms-race.

TED. "How Twitter Needs to Change | Jack Dorsey.'" June 7, 2019. Video, 25:47. https://www.youtube.com/watch?v=Bcg-DvEdGEXg.

World Health Organization Regional Office for Europe. "Milestones for Health Over 70 Years." Accessed February 18, 2021. https://www.euro.who.int/en/about-us/organization/who-at-70/milestones-for-health-over-70-years.

CHAPTER 3

APS News. "This Month in Physics History." 16, no. 5. (May 2007). https://aps.org/publications/apsnews/200705/physicshistory.cfm.

Encyclopædia Britannica Online, s.v. "James Chadwick." Accessed February 19, 2021. https://www.britannica.com/biography/James-Chadwick.

Cartwright, Vanessa. "Futurist, Futurologist, Foresight Practitioner, Visionary, Foresighteer: What's in a Name?" Ross Dawson, June 2, 2015. https://rossdawson.com/futurist-futurologist-foresight-practitioner-visionary-foresighteer-whats-in-a-name/.

McGonical, Jane. "Games—Play Me." Jane McGonigal. Accessed February 19, 2021. https://janemcgonigal.com/play-me/.

Morgan, Blake. "50 Leading Female Futurists." *Forbes*, March 5, 2020. https://www.forbes.com/sites/blakemorgan/2020/03/05/50-leading-female-futurists/?sh=4a5884658c90.

Sandberg, Anders. "AI, Aliens, and Existential Risk with Anders Sandberg." Interview by Ryan O'Shea. *Future Grind*, May 20, 2019. Audio, 1:09:15. https://futuregrind.org/podcast-episodes/2019/5/20/ep-37-ai-aliens-and-existential-risk-with-anders-sandberg.

Sommers, Cecily. *Think Like a Futurist: Know what Changes, What Doesn't and What's Next*. San Francisco: Jossey-Bass, 2012.

Singularity University. "Pablos Holman | Automating Ourselves | Global Summit 2018 | Singularity University." September 16, 2018. Video, 32:57. https://www.youtube.com/watch?app=desktop&v=v233_FKMgm8.

TEDx Talks. "Foresight 101. Designing Our Own Futures | Stuart Candy | TEDxBlackRockCity." January 9, 2015. Video, 15:19. https://www.youtube.com/watch?v=PCEbPhbmbQY.

TEDx Talks. "Inventing the Impossible: Pablos Holman at TEDxUCSD." June 4, 2013. Video, 16:48. https://www.youtube.com/watch?app=desktop&v=v233_FKMgm8.

Ted Talks. "Gaming Can Make a Better World | Jane McGonigal." March 17, 2010. Video, 20:31. https://www.youtube.com/watch?app=desktop&v=dE1DuBesGYM.

PART 2 EPIGRAPH

SxSW EDU. "Jane McGonigal | SXSWedu Keynote | How to Think (and Learn) Like a Futurist." March 9, 2016. Video, 1:08:59.

CHAPTER 4

Badminton, Nikolas. "Consulting." Nikolas Badminton. Accessed February 16, 2021. https://nikolasbadminton.com/consulting.

Chang, Dion. "Trend Release: The State We're In—6 Trend Pillars for 2021." FLUX Trends. Accessed February, 2021. https://www.fluxtrends.com/trend-release-the-state-were-in-6-trend-pillars-for-2021/.

Gosnell, Ken. "Environment Scanning: How CEOS Can Stay Ahead of the Curve and Beat the Competition." *Business.com*. January 24, 2020. https://www.business.com/articles/what-is-environmental-scanning/.

International Futures Forum. "Three Horizons—The Approach." Accessed February 16, 2021. https://www.iffpraxis.com/3h-approach.

Merriam-Webster Dictionary Online. s.v. "signal." Accessed February 16, 2021. https://www.merriam-webster.com/dictionary/signal.

Shah, Baiju and John Green. "How Marketers Can Deal with Disruptors." Fjord, May 20, 2015. https://www.fjordnet.com/conversations/channeling-liquid-expectations/.

Sommers, Cecily. *Think Like a Futurist: Know what Changes, What Doesn't and What's Next.* San Francisco: Jossey-Bass, 2012.

Synn, Anastasia. "The Magic of Biohacking with Anastasia Synn." Interview by Ryan O'Shea. *Future Grind.* Audio, 41:30. https://futuregrind.org/podcast-episodes/2019/8/27/ep-42-the-magic-of-biohacking-with-anastasia-synn.

UNDP Global Centre for Public Service Excellence. "The Use of Strategic Foresight for Adaptive and Future-Ready SDG Strategies." July 17, 2018. Video, 2:54:12. https://www.youtube.com/watch?v=1dQMDitiAw0&t=974s.

Webb, Amy. *The Signals are Talking: Why Today's Fringe Is Tomorrow's Mainstream.* New York: PublicAffairs, 2016.

CHAPTER 5

AAA Hopon Las Vegas. "AAA Free Self-Driving Shuttle Pilot Program." Accessed February 22, 2021. http://www.aaahoponlasvegas.com/.

BIE Paris. "All World Expos." Accessed February 22, 2021. https://www.bie-paris.org/site/en/all-world-expos.

Biesiada, Jamie. "Evolving Epcot." *Travel Weekly.* Accessed February 22, 2021. https://www.travelweekly.com/Travel-News/Hotel-News/Evolving-Epcot.

Captain, Sean. "Mission Impossible: The Ridiculous Tech of Jason Bourne." *Fast Company,* August 2, 2016. https://www.fastcompany.com/3062417/mission-impossible-the-ridiculous-tech-of-jason-bourne.

Delta Corporation. "CES 2020." Accessed February 16, 2021. https://news.delta.com/category/ces-2020.

Disney Corporation. "Unlock the Magic with Your MagicBand or Card." Accessed February 22, 2021. https://disneyworld.disney.go.com/plan/my-disney-experience/bands-cards.

Futurism Creative. "These Recent Sci-fi Books Should Be at the Top of Your Reading List." *Futurism,* January 16, 2019. https://futurism.com/science-fiction-fan-sci-fi-books.

Empathy Museum. "A Mile in My Shoes." Accessed February 16, 2021. https://www.empathymuseum.com/a-mile-in-my-shoes/.

Empathy Museum. "Human Library." Accessed February 16, 2021. https://www.empathymuseum.com/a-mile-in-my-shoes/.

Expo 2021 Dubai. "Expo 2021 Dubai Main Highlights." Accessed February 22, 2021. https://expo-2021-dubai.com/expo-2021-main-highlight/.

Holman, Pablos. "Futurist & Hacker Reveals How to Solve World's Biggest Problems." Interview by Patrick Bet-David. *Valuetainment.* October 23, 2020. Video, 1:17:41. https://www.youtube.com/watch?v=_HuwgMlbpYY&t=843s.

Friend or Follow. "Twitter: Most Followers." Accessed on February 22, 2021. https://friendorfollow.com/twitter/most-followers/.

Hoffman, Jordan. "23 of James Bond's Most Memorable Gadgets." *Popular Mechanics,* October 15, 2012. https://www.popularmechanics.com/culture/movies/g985/23-most-memorable-james-bond-gadgets/.

Hoffman, Jordan. "The 10 Best 'Mission: Impossible' Gadgets." *Popular Mechanics,* June 23, 2018. https://www.popularmechanics.com/culture/movies/g22365901/best-mission-impossible-gadgets.

IESE Business School. "These are the 10 Smartest Cities in the World for 2020." *Forbes,* July 8, 2020. https://www.forbes.com/

sites/iese/2020/07/08/these-are-the-10-smartest-cities-in-the-world-for-2020/?sh=5cdb9af012af.

IMDB. "Top Rated Movies Top 250 as Rated by IMDb Users." Accessed February 19, 2021. https://www.imdb.com/chart/top.

Mossesgeld, Rico. "The Dream-Sharing Technology of Inception." *Tom's Guide,* July 20, 2010. https://www.tomsguide.com/us/inception-dream-sharing,news-7510.html.

Marriott. "Find Your Personal Retreat at Our Marco Island Beach Resort." Access February 22, 2021. https://www.marriott.com/hotels/travel/mrkfl-jw-marriott-marco-island-beach-resort/.

McCluskey, Megan. "17 Times *The Simpsons* Accurately Predicted the Future." *Time.* Last updated June 3, 2020. https://time.com/4667462/simpsons-predictions-donald-trump-lady-gaga/.

Nagy, Attila. "10 *James Bond* Gadgets That Actually Exist—And One That Needs To." *Gizmodo,* December 17, 2012. https://gizmodo.com/10-james-bond-gadgets-that-actually-exist-and-one-that-5966242.

Nanalyze. "7 Robot Baristas That Will Make You Coffee." March 23, 2019. https://www.nanalyze.com/2019/03/robot-baristas/.

Nykamp, Chad and Cindy Nykamp. "The NEW Epcot—Everything You Need to Know About the Transformation of Epcot." *Disney Lists.* Accessed February 22, 2021. https://www.disneylists.com/2020/11/the-new-epcot-everything-you-need-to-know-about-the-transformation-of-epcot-2/.

Princess Cruises. "Princess Medallion Class." Accessed February 22, 2021. https://www.princess.com/ships-and-experience/ocean-medallion/medallionnet/.

Royal Carribean. "Robot Bartenders Shake Things Up at Sea." Accessed February 22, 2021. https://www.royalcaribbean.com/blog/robot-bartenders-shake-things-up-at-sea/.

Soule, Charles. "The Oracle Year." CharlesSoule.com. Accessed February 22, 2021. https://www.charlessoule.com/theoracle-year.

Superflux. "Mitigation of Shock (Singapore)." Accessed February 22, 2021. https://superflux.in/index.php/work/mitigation-of-shock-singapore/.

Truitt, Brian. "Book Revie: The Punch Escrow." *USA Today,* August 1, 2017. https://www.usatoday.com/story/life/books/2017/08/01/book-review-the-punch-escrow/525089001/.

Wright, Mindy. "Revealed: Countries with the Fastest Internet Speeds, 2020." *CEO World Biz.* February 21, 2020. https://ceoworld.biz/2020/02/21/revealed-countries-with-the-fastest-internet-speeds-2020/.

Yotel HQ. "Hotel or YOTEL?" November 15, 2019. Video, 0:31. https://www.youtube.com/watch?app=desktop&v=0F3R8ygsWug&feature=emb_title.

CHAPTER 6

Alba, Davey. "It's Your Fault Microsoft's Teen AI Turned into Such a Jerk." *Wired,* March 25, 2016. https://www.wired.com/2016/03/fault-microsofts-teen-ai-turned-jerk/.

Bank of England. "Alan Turing to Be the Face of New £50 Note." July 15, 2019. https://www.bankofengland.co.uk/news/2019/july/50-pound-banknote-character-announcement.

BBC. "AI: 15 Key Moments in the Story of Artificial Intelligence." Accessed February 22, 2021. https://www.bbc.co.uk/teach/ai-15-key-moments-in-the-story-of-artificial-intelligence/zh77cqt.

Bertscheler, Joey. "CRISPR: Its Potential and Concerns in the Genetic Engineering Field." *Forbes.* March 9, 2020. https://www.forbes.com/sites/theyec/2020/03/09/crispr-its-potential-and-concerns-in-the-genetic-engineering-field/?sh=764585b113ca.

Biography Magazine. "Alan Turing Biography." Last updated July 22, 2020. https://www.biography.com/scientist/alan-turing.

British Pathé. "Mechanical Tortoise (1951)." Aug 27, 2014. Video, 2:19. https://www.youtube.com/watch?v=wQE82derooc.

Broad Institute. "CRISPR Timeline." Accessed February 23, 2021. https://www.broadinstitute.org/what-broad/areas-focus/project-spotlight/crispr-timeline.

Chen, Rosalie. "What to Know About Gordie Howe's Controversial Stem Cell Treatment." Time. June 10, 2016. https://time.com/4364238/gordie-howe-stem-cell-treatment/.

Cho, Wendy K Tam, and Bruce E. Cain. "Human-centered Redistricting Automation in the Age of AI." Science Magazine 369, no. 6508 (September 4, 2020): 1179-1181. DOI: 10.1126/science.abd1879.

Colwell, Brian. "Biotechnology timeline: Humans Have Manipulated Genes Since the 'Dawn of Civilization'." Genetic Literacy Project, September 8, 2020. https://geneticliteracyproject.org/2020/09/08/biotechnology-timeline-humans-manipulating-genes-since-dawn-civilization/.

Delta Impact. "Electronic Tattoos Uses and Benefits." Accessed February 22, 2021. https://www.deltaimpact.com/blog/electronic-tattoos-uses-and-benefits/.

DNA Worldwide. "The History of DNA Timeline." Accessed February 22, 2012. https://www.dna-worldwide.com/resource/160/history-dna-timeline.

Drews, Frank A. and Jonathan R. Zadra. "The Human-Technology Interface." Oxford Medicine Online, October 2016. DOI:10.1093/med/9780199366149.003.0004.

Envisionoptics. "Electronic Eyeglasses and Electronic Contacts." Accessed February 22, 2021. https://www.evisionoptics.com/electronic-eyeglasses-electronic-contacts/.

Ganer, Heidi. "Real-Life X-Men: How CRISPR Could Give You Superpowers in the Future." *SyntheGo.* September 14, 2018. https://www.synthego.com/blog/could-crispr-make-x-men-a-realistic-possibility.

Grudin, Robert. s.v. "Humanism." *Encyclopædia Britannica Online.* Accessed February 22, 2012, https://www.britannica.com/topic/humanism.

Hanson Robotics. "Sophia." Accessed February 22, 2012. https://www.hansonrobotics.com/sophia/.

Hayes, Sean A. s.v. "Transhumanism." *Encyclopædia Britannica Online.* Accessed February 22, 2021, https://www.britannica.com/topic/transhumanism.

Heath, Nick. "What is AI? Everything You Need to Know About Artificial Intelligence." *ZDNet,* December 11, 2020. https://www.zdnet.com/article/what-is-ai-everything-you-need-to-know-about-artificial-intelligence/.

Joshi, Naveen. "7 Types of Artificial Intelligence." *Forbes,* June 19, 2019. https://www.forbes.com/sites/cognitiveworld/2019/06/19/7-types-of-artificial-intelligence/?sh=37f03822233e.

Kingma, Luke. "Glimpes: How Electronic Tattoos Will Change the World—and Ourselves." *Futurism,* September 17, 2018. https://futurism.com/glimpse-electronic-tattoos.

Gerd Leonhard. "Transhumanist Calum Chace and Humanist Gerd Leonhard Live Debate (TheFutureShow)." April 23, 2020. Video, 1:25:49. https://www.youtube.com/watch?v=ZFN6jHeky4Y.

Metzl, Jamie. "Joe Rogan Experience #1294—Jamie Metzl." Interview by Joe Rogan. *The Joe Rogan Experience,* May 10, 2019.

Audio, 2:29:00. https://www.jrepodcast.com/episode/joe-rogan-experience-1294-jamie-metzl/.

Metzl, Jamie. "Human Genetics Engineering and the Catholic Church." July 24, 2020. https://jamiemetzl.com/human-genetic-engineering-and-the-catholic-church/.

MIT. "Kismet: A Robot for Social Interactions with Humans." 1998. http://www.ai.mit.edu/projects/kismet-new/kismet.html.

Morris, Andrea. "We Need to Talk About Sentient Robots." *Forbes,* March 13, 2018. https://www.forbes.com/sites/andreamorris/2018/03/13/we-need-to-talk-about-sentient-robots/?sh=6779f8b71b2c.

Morrow, Jamie. "'Silicon Valley,' Season 5, Episode 5—AI Robot Doesn't Like Her Human Creator." *Daily Post,* April 22, 2018. https://padailypost.com/2018/04/22/silicon-valley-season-5-episode-5-ai-robot-doesnt-like-her-human-creator/.

Neiger, Chris. "6 Scary Stories of AI Gone Wrong." *The Motley Fool.* October 31, 2017. https://www.fool.com/investing/2017/10/31/6-scary-stories-of-ai-gone-wrong.aspx.

Oppy, Graham and David Dowe. "The Turing Test." *Stanford Encyclopedia of Philosophy.* Last updated August 18, 2020. https://plato.stanford.edu/entries/turing-test/.

Pease, Rolan. "Alan Turing: Inquest's Suicide Verdict 'Not Supportable'." *BBC.* June 26, 2012. https://www.bbc.com/news/science-environment-18561092.

Olivia Solon. "Alan Turing's Extraordinary, Tragically Short Life: A Timeline." *Wired,* June 18, 2012. https://www.wired.com/2012/06/alan-turing-timeline/.

Reid, David. "Google's DeepMind A.I. Beats Doctors in Breast Cancer Screening Trial." *CNBC,* January 2, 2020. https://www.cnbc.com/2020/01/02/googles-deepmind-ai-beats-doctors-in-breast-cancer-screening-trial.html.

Salk Institute. "CRISPR/Cas9 Therapy can Suppress Aging, Enhance Health and Extend Life Span in Mice." *Science Daily,* February 19, 2019. https://www.sciencedaily.com/releases/2019/02/190219111747.htm.

Salonga, Bianca. "Bio Hacking: The Key to Endless Energy and Aging in Reverse." *Forbes,* February 28, 2020. https://www.forbes.com/sites/biancasalonga/2020/02/28/bio-hacking-the-key-to-endless-energy-and-aging-in-reverse/?sh=7666172021ef.

Sample, Ian. "Chinese Scientist Who Edited Babies' Genes Jailed for Three Years." *The Guardian,* December 30, 2019. https://www.theguardian.com/world/2019/dec/30/gene-editing-chinese-scientist-he-jiankui-jailed-three-years.

Schmidt, Charles. "Genetic Engineering Could Make a COVID-19 Vaccine in Months Rather Than Years Candidates are speeding toward human trials." *Scientific American,* June 1, 2020. https://www.scientificamerican.com/article/genetic-engineering-could-make-a-covid-19-vaccine-in-months-rather-than-years1/.

Shankland, Stephen and Jackson Ryan. "Elon Musk Shows Neuralink Brain Implant Working in a Pig." *c|net,* August 29, 2020. https://www.cnet.com/news/elon-musk-shows-neuralink-brain-implant-working-in-a-pig/.

Shead, Sam. "Researchers: Are We on the Cusp of an 'AI Winter'?" *BBC News,* January 12, 2020. https://www.bbc.com/news/technology-51064369.

Shead, Sam. "Elon Musk Says His Start-up Neuralink has Wired Up a Monkey to Play Video Games Using Its Mind." *CNBC,* February 1, 2021. https://www.cnbc.com/2021/02/01/elon-musk-neuralink-wires-up-monkey-to-play-video-games-using-mind.html.

Simplilearn. "Types of Artificial Intelligence | Artificial Intelligence Explained | What Is AI?" August 23, 2020. Video, 9:25. https://www.youtube.com/watch?v=VNz3KG0AhG4.

Simon, Matt. "Inside the Amazon Warehouse Where Humans and Machines Become One." *Wired*, June 5, 2019. https://www.wired.com/story/amazon-warehouse-robots/.

Solon, Olivia. "The Ratio Club: A Melting Pot for British Cybernetics." *Wired*, June 21, 2012. https://www.wired.co.uk/article/ratio-club-turing.

Swelitz, Ika. "Squishy Embryos, Penis Transplants, and 5 More Advances in Fertility Treatment." *STAT*, March 6, 2016. https://www.statnews.com/2016/03/10/new-fertility-treatments/.

SXSW. "Amy Webb's Emerging Tech Trends for 2020." May 6, 2020, video, 1:00:10. https://www.youtube.com/watch?app=desktop&v=uoD5M66p3yU.

Synced AI Technology & Industry Review. "2018 in Review: 10 AI Failures." December 10, 2018. https://medium.com/syncedreview/2018-in-review-10-ai-failures-c18faadf5983.

Synn, Anastasia. "The Magic of Biohacking with Anastasia Synn." Interview by Ryan O'Shea. *Future Grind*. Audio, 41:30. https://futuregrind.org/podcast-episodes/2019/8/27/ep-42-the-magic-of-biohacking-with-anastasia-synn.

Tangermann, Victor. "Stores in Japan Are Stocking Shelves with Remote-controlled Robots." *Futurism*, September 15, 2020.

Trenholm, Richard. "Apple Maps Mishap Sees Drivers Crash Airport Runway." *c|net*, September 26, 2013. https://www.cnet.com/news/apple-maps-mishap-sees-drivers-crash-airport-runway/.

Webb, Amy. *The Big Nine: How the Tech Titans and Their Thinking Machines Could Warp Humanity*. New York: PublicAffairs, 2019.

CHAPTER 7

3M. "America's Top Young Scientist of 2020: 14-Year-Old Researches Spike Protein of SARS-CoV-2 Virus to Develop Novel Antiviral Drug to Combat Spread of COVID-19." *Business Wire,* October 14, 2020. https://www.businesswire.com/news/home/20201014005340/en/.

Accenture Digital. "Accenture Interactive Manifesto." October 25, 2018. Video, 1:13.

Coyne, Marley. "This See-Through Mask Lets the Deaf Communicate While Staying Safe." *Forbes,* April 4, 2020. https://www.forbes.com/sites/marleycoyne/2020/04/04/this-see-through-mask-lets-the-deaf-communicate-while-staying-safe/?sh=682f86865257.

Department of Economic and Social Affairs Sustainable Development. "The 17 Goals." *United Nations.* Accessed February 22, 2021. https://sdgs.un.org/goals.

Dimon, Jamie. "Jamie Dimon—Chairman and CEO of JPMorgan Chase." Interview by Miles Fisher, *Coffee with The Greats,* July 2020. Audio, 1:06:50. https://anchor.fm/blamo-media/episodes/Jamie-Dimon---Chairman-and-CEO-of-JPMorgan-Chase-egn5as.

Gable, John. "How the Internet Trains our Brains to Polarize and Despise." *Allsides,* November 27, 2012. https://www.allsides.com/blog/internet-trains-brains-polarize-despise.

Moss, David A. "Fixing What's Wrong with Politics." *Harvard Business Review,* March 2012. https://hbr.org/2012/03/fixing-whats-wrong-with-us-politics.

Satel, Sally. "Inside the Controversy over 'the Chinese Virus'." *National Review,* March 23, 2020. https://www.nationalreview.com/2020/03/inside-the-controversy-over-the-chinese-virus/.

"Saudi Ideological War Center Launches Initiatives to Fight Terrorism." *Arab News*, May 2, 2017. https://www.arabnews.com/node/1093386/saudi-arabia.

Shinde, Jayesh. "Meet Haaziq Kazi, 12-Year-Old From Pune Who Designed A Ship That Can Clean And Save Our Oceans." *India Times*, November 24, 2018, https://www.indiatimes.com/technology/news/meet-haaziq-kazi-12-year-old-from-pune-who-designed-a-ship-that-can-clean-and-save-our-oceans-357277.html.

Ted-Ed Student Talks. "Cleaning our Oceans: A Big Plan for a Big Problem." March 9, 2018. Video, 10:52. https://www.youtube.com/watch?v=v4-arqhTszc.

Thawer, Ejaz. "The Terminology of Terrorism: Why Naming Matters in Ideological Warfare." *Centre for International and Defence Policy*, June 24, 2019. https://medium.com/centre-for-international-and-defence-policy/the-terminology-of-terrorism-why-naming-matters-in-ideological-warfare-7831d8fec64b.

Weiss, Jessica Chen. "Are the United States and China in an Ideological Competition?" Center for Strategic and *International Studies*, December 13, 2019. https://www.csis.org/blogs/freeman-chair-blog/are-united-states-and-china-ideological-competition.

PART 3 EPIGRAPH

Pinker, Steven. *Enlightenment Now*. New York: Penguin Random House, 2018.

CHAPTER 8

Candy, Stuart. "Thing from the Future Card Game." November 11, 2014. Video, 20:29. https://vimeo.com/111582424.

Candy, Stuart and Jeff Watson. "The Thing from the Future." Situation Lab. Accessed February 1, 2020. https://situationlab.org/project/the-thing-from-the-future/.

Cotton, Martha. "Three Is for Impactful Design Research." *Design Voices,* November 8, 2017. https://medium.com/design-voices/three-i-s-for-impactful-design-research-9bd41929c3eb.

Google Design. "Design is [Protopian]." May 17, 2019, video, 1:00:49. https://www.youtube.com/watch?v=ixg7e1fWdMo.

Klein, Naomi. "A Message from the Future with Alexandria Ocasio-Cortez." *The Intercept,* April 17, 2019. https://theintercept.com/2019/04/17/green-new-deal-short-film-alexandria-ocasio-cortez/.

Saffo, Paul. "Six Rules for Effective Forecasting." *Harvard Business Review,* July–August 2007. https://hbr.org/2007/07/six-rules-for-effective-forecasting.

SxSW EDU. "Jane McGonigal | SXSWedu Keynote | How to Think (and Learn) Like a Futurist." March 9, 2016. Video, 1:08:59. https://www.youtube.com/watch?v=CKvMmtclUBA&t=2071s.

Webb, Amy. *The Signals are Talking: Why Today's Fringe Is Tomorrow's Mainstream.* New York: PublicAffairs, 2016.

UNDP Global Centre for Public Service Excellence. "The Use of Strategic Foresight for Adaptive and Future-Ready SDG Strategies." July 17, 2018. Video, 2:54:12. https://www.youtube.com/watch?v=1dQMDitiAw0&t=974s.

Webb, Amy. "The Tech Trends You Need to Know For 2016." LinkedIn, December 8, 2015. https://www.linkedin.com/pulse/tech-trends-you-need-know-2016-amy-webb/.

CHAPTER 9

Corning Incorporated. "A Day Made of Glass…Made Possible by Corning. (2011)." February 7, 2011. Video, 5:32. https://www.youtube.com/watch?app=desktop&v=6Cf7IL_eZ38.

Diamond, Jared. *Collapse: How Societies Choose to Fail or Succeed.* New York: Penguin Books, 2011.

Dufva, Mikko. "The Horizon Scanning Zoo." *Ennakointikupla.* Accessed February 24, 2021. https://www.ennakointikupla.fi/blog/index.php/2016/04/11/the-horizon-scanning-zoo.

Graham, David A. "Rumsfeld's Knowns and Unknowns: The Intellectual History of a Quip." *The Atlantic,* March 27, 2014. https://www.theatlantic.com/politics/archive/2014/03/rumsfelds-knowns-and-unknowns-the-intellectual-history-of-a-quip/359719/.

Jain, Anab. "Why We Need to Imagine Different Futures." Filmed April 2017 in Vancouver, B.C. TED video, 14:31. https://www.ted.com/talks/anab_jain_why_we_need_to_imagine_different_futures.

Sardar, Ziauddin and John A. Sweeney. "The Three Tomorrows of Postnormal Times." *Futures* 75 (2016):1-13. //doi.org/10.1016/j.futures.2015.10.004.

CHAPTER 10

Frasier. "Fraternal Schwinns." Season 10, Episode 16. February 25, 2003. Directed by Sheldon Epps, Paramount. Video, 21:00. https://www.paramountplus.com/shows/frasier/video/95CFF39C-A17E-5CB0-57F0-A229A0BA67EE/frasier-fraternal-schwinns/.

Heshmat, Shahram. "The Scarcity Mindset: How Does Being Poor Change the Way We Feel and Think?" *Psychology Today,* April 2, 2015. https://www.psychologytoday.com/us/blog/science-choice/201504/the-scarcity-mindset.

Kelly, Kevin. *The Inevitable: Understanding the 12 Technological Forces That Will Shape Our Future.* United Kingdom: Penguin Books, 2017.

Jain, Anab and Jon Ardern. "Stark Choices." Superflux, 2018. Accessed February 21, 2021. https://superflux.in/index.php/work/stark-choices/#.

Sommers, Cecily. *Think Like a Futurist: Know what Changes, What Doesn't and What's Next.* San Francisco: Jossey-Bass, 2012.

TEDx Talks. "Foresight 101. Designing our own futures | Stuart Candy | TEDxBlackRockCity." January 9, 2015. Video, 15:19. https://www.youtube.com/watch?v=PCEbPhbmbQY.

PART 4 EPIGRAPH

Taket, Ann, ed. "Health Futures in Support of Health for All." World Health Organization. July 19-23, 1993. https://apps.who.int/iris/bitstream/handle/10665/61479/WHO_HST_93.4_eng.pdf;sequence=1.

CHAPTER 11

Beardsley, Tim. "Strategic Defense Initiative: Star Wars criticized by OTA report." *Nature* 317, no. 6035 (September 1985). https://doi.org/10.1038/317276a0.

British Ecological Society. "Top 10 Tips for Engaging and Communicating with Policymakers." Accessed February 16, 2021. https://www.britishecologicalsociety.org/wp-content/uploads/Top-10-tips-for-effectively-engaging-and-communicating-with-policy-makers.pdf.

Bulletin of the Atomic Scientists. "This is Your COVID Wake-up Call: It is 100 Seconds to Midnight." *Bulletin of the Atomic Scientists,* January 27, 2021. Video, 1:01:51. https://thebulletin.org/doomsday-clock/current-time/.

Dimon, Jamie. "Jamie Dimon—Chairman and CEO of JPMorgan Chase." interview by Miles Fisher, *Coffee with The Greats,* July 2020. Audio, 1:06:50. https://anchor.fm/blamo-media/episodes/

Jamie-Dimon---Chairman-and-CEO-of-JPMorgan-Chase-egn5as.

Gedye, Grace. "How Congress Got Dumb on Tech—and How It Can Get Smart." *Washington Monthly*, April-June 2019. https://washingtonmonthly.com/magazine/april-may-june-2019/how-congress-got-dumb-on-tech-and-how-it-can-get-smart/.

Goodwin, Marie. "The Four Levels: New Story Activism and Burnout." *Resilience*, August 17, 2016. https://www.resilience.org/stories/2016-08-17/the-four-levels-new-story-activism-burnout/.

Holt, Rush. "Statement of the Representative Holt on the Office of Technology Assessment." The House of Representatives, February 14, 2009. https://ota.fas.org/reports/AAAS-holt.pdf.

House Energy Subcommittees on Environment and Digital Commerca & Consumer Protection hearing. "Quantum Computing." Streamed by CSPAN, May 18, 2018. Video, 1:22:00. https://www.c-span.org/video/?445771-1/house-panel-explores-benefits-quantum-computing.

Jain, Anab. "Why We Need to Imagine Different Futures." Filmed April 2017, Vancouver, B.C. TED video, 14:31. https://www.ted.com/talks/anab_jain_why_we_need_to_imagine_different_futures.

Monica Anderson, Skye Toor, Lee Rainie and Aaron Smith. "Public attitudes toward political engagement on social media." Pew Research Center, July 11, 2018. https://www.pewresearch.org/internet/2018/07/11/public-attitudes-toward-political-engagement-on-social-media/.

Oremus, Will. "Google's Web of Confusion." *Slate*, December 11, 2018. https://slate.com/technology/2018/12/google-congress-hearing-sundar-pichai-confusion-regulation.html.

Park, Andrea. "2020 Voter Turnout Was the Highest the US Has Seen in Over a Century." *Marie Claire*, November 5, 2020.

https://www.marieclaire.com/politics/a34589422/voter-turnout-2020/.

Piazza, Alessandro. "Firm Behavior and Evolution of Activism: Strategic Decisions and the Emergence of Protest in US Communities." *Strategic Management Journal* 41, no. 4 (November 26, 2019). https://doi.org/10.1002/smj.3116.

Rampton, John. "20 Life Changing Quotes by Tony Robbins." *Inc*, July 25, 2016. https://www.inc.com/john-rampton/20-life-changing-quotes-by-tony-robbins.html.

Rosenblatt, Gideon. "The Engagement Pyramid: Six Levels of Connecting People and Social Change." *Groundwire*, February 1, 2010. http://groundwire.org/blog/groundwire-engagement-pyramid/.

Sommers, Cecily. *Think Like a Futurist: Know what Changes, What Doesn't and What's Next.* San Francisco: Jossey-Bass. 2012.

Wallace, Gregor. "Voter Turnout at 20-year Low in 2016." *CNN*, November 30, 2016. https://www.cnn.com/2016/11/11/politics/popular-vote-turnout-2016/index.html.

Webb, Amy. "A National Office for Strategic Foresight Anchored in Critical Science and Technologies." *Stanford Geopolitics, Technology and Governance* Cyber Policy Center. October 17, 2019. https://fsi-live.s3.us-west-1.amazonaws.com/s3fs-public/webb_sfo_final_0.pdf.

Wexler, Celia. "Bring Back the Office of Technology Assessment." *The New York Times,* May 28, 2015. https://www.nytimes.com/roomfordebate/2015/05/28/scientists-curbing-the-ethical-use-of-science/bring-back-the-office-of-technology-assessment.

Zuckerberg, Mark. "Transcript of Mark Zuckerberg's Senate Hearing." Transcribed by Bloomberg, April 10, 2018. https://www.washingtonpost.com/news/the-switch/wp/2018/04/10/transcript-of-mark-zuckerbergs-senate-hearing/.

CHAPTER 12

Arizona State University. "Consortium for Science, Policy and Outcomes." Accessed February 21, 2021. https://science.asu.edu/consortium-science-policy-and-outcomes.

Arizona State University. "Research Centers." Accessed March 15, 2021. https://cidse.engineering.asu.edu/research-centers/.

Awad, Edmond, Sohan Dsouza, Azim Shariff, Jean-François Bonnefon, Iyad Rahwan MIT Media Lab. "Project Moral Machine." Accessed February 20, 2021. https://www.media.mit.edu/projects/moral-machine/overview/.

Carnegie Mellon University. "Stuart Candy." Accessed March 15, 2021. https://www.design.cmu.edu/user/1459.

futuribles. "Who Are We?" Accessed March 15, 2021. https://www.futuribles.com/en/qui-sommes-nous/.

reelblack. "The Futurists (1967) | Scientists Predict the 21st Century." December 15, 2018. Video, 25:11. https://www.youtube.com/watch?v=wPETzKYLkc0&t=198s.

Tedx Talks. "Foresight 101. Designing Our Own Futures | Stuart Candy | TEDxBlackRockCity." January 9, 2015. Video, 15:19. https://www.youtube.com/watch?v=PCEbPhbmbQY.

University of Hawai'i, Department of Political Science, College of Social Sciences. "Alternative Futures." Mānoa. https://politicalscience.manoa.hawaii.edu/.

University of Houston, College of Technology, Foresight Program. "Program." Accessed February 21, 2021. https://www.houstonforesight.org/program.

Webb, Amy. "The Big Nine: The Future of AI." Filmed at Columbia Business School. August 15, 2019. Video, 23:01. https://www.youtube.com/watch?v=S2tmo_18fyo.

World Futures Studies Federation. "WFSF in Brief." Accessed February 1, 2021.

CHAPTER 13

Chopyak, Jill, Peter and Levesque. "Public Participation in Science and Technology Decision Making: Trends for the Future." *Technology in Society* 24, no. 1-2 (2002): 155-166. DOI:10.1016/S0160-791X(01)00051-3.

Eswaran, Vijay. "The Business Case for Diversity in the Workplace is Now Overwhelming." *World Economic Forum,* April 29, 2019. https://www.weforum.org/agenda/2019/04/business-case-for-diversity-in-the-workplace/.

Equity Institute. "Equity Audit Window." Accessed February 20, 2021. https://www.equity.institute/window.

Georgette Zinaty. "High Five: Making the Pivot Part of Your Quintuple Bottom Line." *Forbes*, December 28, 2020. https://www.forbes.com/sites/forbescoachescouncil/2021/12/28/high-five-making-the-pivot-part-of-your-quintuple-bottom-line/?sh=7ef74c2650b1.

Gerd Leonhard. "Ten Essential Future Foresights for a Post Corona World: A Covid-19 Virtual Keynote by Gerd Leonhard." June 22, 2020. Video, 47:48. https://www.youtube.com/watch?v=lB-MGZhHfCFw.

Harvard Business Review Analytic Services. "The Business Case for Purpose." 2015. https://assets.ey.com/content/dam/ey-sites/ey-com/en_gl/topics/digital/ey-the-business-case-for-purpose.pdf.

Hassan, Lobna. Governments Should Play Games: Towards a Framework for the Gamification of Civic Engagement Platforms. *Simulation and Gaming* 48, no 2 (2017): 249-267. DOI: 10.1177/1046878116683581.

Merriam-Webster Dictionary Online. s.v. "inclusion." Accessed March 16, 2021. https://www.merriam-webster.com/dictionary/inclusion.

Metzl, Jamie. "Joe Rogan Experience #1294—Jamie Metzl." Interview by Joe Rogan. *The Joe Rogan Experience*, May 10, 2019. Audio, 2:29:00. https://www.jrepodcast.com/episode/joe-rogan-experience-1294-jamie-metzl/.

Martinuzzi, André, Vincent Blok, Alexander Brem, Bernd Stahl, Norma Schönherr. "Responsible Research and Innovation in Industry—Challenges, Insights and Perspectives." *Sustainability* 10, no. 3. (2018): 702. https://doi.org/10.3390/su10030702.

Nazarko, Lukasz. "Responsible Research and Innovation—a Conceptual Contribution to Theory and Practice of Technology Management." *Business: Theory and Practice* 20. (August 2019):342-51. https://doi.org/10.3846/btp.2019.32.

O'Brien, Michael J. "Most D&I Programs are Ineffective. Here's How to Change That." *Human Resource Executive*. November 5, 2019. https://hrexecutive.com/most-di-programs-are-ineffective-heres-how-to-change-that/.

Paul R. La Monica. "Innovative Companies are Trouncing the Rest of the Market." *CNN Business*, May 20, 2019. https://www.cnn.com/2019/05/20/investing/innovation-index-stocks/index.html.

Priya Merchant. "Pivoting During the Pandemic: How These Businesses Succeeded." *Entrepreneur*, January 12, 2021. https://www.entrepreneur.com/article/362003.

Project Management Institute. "The Bottom Line on Sustainability." 2011. Accessed February 20, 2021. https://www.pmi.org/-/media/pmi/documents/public/pdf/white-papers/the-bottom-line-on-sustanability.pdf.

Stanford Alumni. "Developing a Growth Mindset with Carol Dweck." October 9, 2014. Video, 9:37. https://www.youtube.com/watch?v=hiiEeMN7vbQ.

TEDx Talks, "TEDxPerth—Jason Clarke—Embracing Change." December 22, 2010. Video, 18:03. https://www.youtube.com/watch?v=vPhM8lxibSU.

Tonn, Bruce Edward, and Dorian Stiefel. "Anticipating the Unanticipated-Unintended Consequences of Scientific and Technological Purposive Actions." *World Futures Review* 11, no. 1 (March 2019): 19–50. https://doi.org/10.1177/1946756718789413.

Tulshyan, Ruchika. "Racially Diverse Companies Outperform Industry Norms by 35%." *Forbes,* January 20, 2015. https://www.forbes.com/sites/ruchikatulshyan/2015/01/30/racially-diverse-companies-outperform-industry-norms-by-30/?sh=-1c8a7c9d1132.

The Vernā Meyers Company. "Diversity Doesn't Stick Without Inclusion." February 4, 2017. https://www.vernamyers.com/2017/02/04/diversity-doesnt-stick-without-inclusion/.

CHAPTER 14

Cameron, Elizabeth E., ed., Jennifer B. Nuzzo, ed., Jessica A. Bell, ed. "2019 Global Health Security Index." *Global Health Security Index.* https://www.ghsindex.org/wp-content/uploads/2020/04/2019-Global-Health-Security-Index.pdf.

Ceicyte, Jolita and Monika Petraite. "Networked Responsibility Approach for Responsible Innovation: Perspective of the Firm." *Sustainability (Switzerland)* 10, no. 6 (March 18, 2018): 1720. https://doi.org/10.3390/su10061720.

Chopyak, Jill, and Peter Levesque. "Public Participation in Science and Technology Decision Making: Trends for the Future." *Technology in Society* 25 (2002): 155-166. https://doi.org/10.1016/S0160-791X(01)00051-3.

Cronck, Terri Moon. "DOD Innovation Speed Must Increase to Modernize." *DOD News,* August 7, 2020. https://www.defense.

gov/Explore/News/Article/Article/2305705/dod-innovation-speed-must-increase-to-modernize/.

Habegger, Beat. "Strategic Foresight in Public Policy: Reviewing the Experiences of the UK, Singapore, and the Netherlands." *Futures* 42, no. 1 (February 2010): 49-58. https://doi.org/10.1016/j.futures.2009.08.002.

Holman, Pablos. "Futurist & Hacker Reveals How To Solve World's Biggest Problems." Interview by Patrick Bet-David. *Valuetainment*, October 23, 2020. Video, 1:17:41. https://www.youtube.com/watch?v=_HuwgMlbpYY&t=843s.

Kullenberg, Christopher and Dick Kasperowski. "What Is Citizen Science?—A Scientometric Meta-Analysis." PLoS One 11, no. 1, (January 2016). DOI:10.1371/journal.pone.0147152.

Gerd Leonhard. "Ten Essential Future Foresights for a Post Corona World: A Covid-19 Virtual Keynote by Gerd Leonhard." June 22, 2020. Video, 47:48. https://www.youtube.com/watch?v=lB-MGZhHfCFw.

Martinuzzi, Andre, Vincent Blok, Alexander Brem, Bernd Stahl, and Norma Schönherr. "Responsible Research and Innovation in Industry-Challenges, Insights and Perspectives." *Sustainability (Switzerland)* 10, no. 3 (2019): 1–10. https://doi.org/10.3390/su10030702.

McGonical, Jane. "Games—Play Me." Jane McGonigal. Accessed February 19, 2021. https://janemcgonigal.com/play-me/.

Nazarko, Lucasz. "Responsible Research and Innovation—A Conceptual Contribution to Theory and Practice of Technology Management." *Business: Theory and Practice* 20 (2019): 342–351. https://doi.org/10.3846/btp.2019.32.

Orszag, Peter R. "Open Government Directive." The White House, December 8, 2009 (memorandum). Accessed February 21, 2021. https://obamawhitehouse.archives.gov/open/documents/open-government-directive.

Owen, Richard. Phil Macnaghten, Jack Stilgoe. "Responsible Research and Innovation: From Science in Society to Science for Society, with Society." *Science and Public Policy* 39, no. 6, (December 2012): 751–760. https://doi.org/10.1093/scipol/scs093.

Pancer, S. Mark. *The Psychology of Citizenship and Civic Engagement*. Oxford: Oxford University Press, 2014.

Parker, Miles, Andrew Acland, Harry J. Armstrong, Jim R. Bellingham, Jessica Bland, Helen C. Bodmer, Simon Burall, Sarah Castell, Jason Chilvers, David D. Cleevely, David Cope, Lucia Costanzo, James A. Dolan, Robert Doubleday, Wai Yi Feng, H. Charles J. Godfray, David A. Good, Jonathan Grant, Nick Green, Arnoud J. Groen, Tim T. Guilliams, Sunjai Gupta, Amanda C. Hall, Adam Heathfield, Ulrike Hotopp, Gary Kass, Tim Leeder, Fiona A. Lickorish, Leila M. Lueshi, Chris Magee, Tiago Mata, Tony McBride, Natasha McCarthy, Alan Mercer, Ross Neilson, Jackie Ouchikh, Edward J. Oughton, David Oxenham, Helen Pallett, James Palmer, Jeff Patmore, Judith Petts, Jan Pinkerton, Richard Ploszek, Alan Pratt, Sophie A. Rocks, Neil Stansfield, Elizabeth Surkovic, Christopher P. Tyler, Andrew R. Watkinson, Jonny Wentworth, Rebecca Willis, Patrick K. A. Wollner, Kim Worts, William J. Sutherland. "Identifying the science and technology dimensions of emerging public policy issues through horizon scanning." *PloS One* 9, no. 5 (May 20, 2014). 10.1371/journal.pone.0096480.

Reuters. "Federal Reserve Chair Jerome Powell Discusses Monetary Policy." August 27, 2020. Video, 58:38. https://www.youtube.com/watch?app=desktop&t=2237&v=LgRwVezt3do&feature=youtu.be.

Tonn, Bruce Edward and Dorian Stiefel. "Anticipating the Unanticipated-Unintended Consequences of Scientific and Technological Purposive Actions." *World Futures Review* 11, no. 1 (August 1, 2018): 19–50. https://doi.org/10.1177/1946756718789413.

UNDP Global Centre for Public Service Excellence. "The Use of Strategic Foresight for Adaptive and Future-Ready SDG Strategies." July 17, 2018. Video, 2:54:12. https://www.youtube.com/watch?v=1dQMDitiAwo&t=974s.

U.S.NRC. "The NRC Approach to Open Government." Accessed February 20, 2021. https://www.nrc.gov/public-involve/open.html.

Wilford, Sara H. "First Line Steps in Requirements Identification for Guidelines Development in Responsible Research and Innovation (RRI)." *Systemic Practice and Action Research* 31, (January 25, 2018): 539-556. https://doi.org/10.1007/s11213-018-9445-z.

Williams, Briana. "Under Trump, US Government Moves from /Open to /Closed." Sunlight Foundation, January 24, 2018. https://sunlightfoundation.com/2018/01/24/under-trump-us-government-moves-from-open-to-closed/.

Williams, Simon N. "A Twenty-First Century Citizens' POLIS: Introducing a Democratic Experiment in Electronic Citizen Participation in Science and Technology Decision-Making." *Public Understanding of Science* 19, no. 5 (September 2010): 528–44. https://doi.org/10.1177/0963662509104726.